Confessions of a Eurosceptic

Confessions of a Eurosceptic

David Heathcoat-Amory

Pen & Sword
POLITICS

First published in Great Britain in 2012 by
PEN & SWORD POLITICS
An imprint of
Pen & Sword Books Ltd
47 Church Street
Barnsley
South Yorkshire
S70 2AS

ISBN 978-1-78159-048-5

Typeset by Concept, Huddersfield, West Yorkshire.
Printed and bound in England by CPI Group (UK) Ltd, Croydon, CR0 4YY.

Pen & Sword Books Ltd incorporates the imprints of Pen & Sword Aviation,
Pen & Sword Family History, Pen & Sword Maritime, Pen & Sword Military,
Pen & Sword Discovery, Wharncliffe Local History, Wharncliffe True Crime,
Wharncliffe Transport, Pen & Sword Select, Pen & Sword Military Classics,
Leo Cooper, The Praetorian Press, Remember When, Seaforth Publishing and
Frontline Publishing.

For a complete list of Pen & Sword titles please contact
PEN & SWORD BOOKS LIMITED
47 Church Street, Barnsley, South Yorkshire, S70 2AS, England
E-mail: enquiries@pen-and-sword.co.uk
Website: www.pen-and-sword.co.uk

Contents

'Is not every meanest day the conflux of two eternities.'

Thomas Carlyle

Foreword

During the twenty-seven years I was a Member of Parliament, our relationship with the European Union was the source of many hopes, fears and failures. It caused constant discord and strife, and contributed to the downfall of two prime ministers. The European question was central to my own career as a backbencher, then as a minister until I resigned, and then again in opposition. It remains an unresolved issue today and has created a new economic crisis.

The story that follows charts my own journey from acceptance of the EU to rejection of it, and my involvement in these controversies as Minister for Europe and as Paymaster General. It is not a history of the subject, but a personal account which illustrates how and why crucial decisions and mistakes were made. We need to understand these mistakes if we are not to repeat them. I shall give proposals for what needs to be done now to create a democratic Europe based on the principles of self-government and international cooperation, or, failing that, a different relationship between Britain and the EU.

It is sometimes alleged that hostility to the EU is driven by blinkered nationalism or xenophobia, but in my case it was the early experiences I had abroad that convinced me of Britain's global responsibilities, and it was often the EU which I found to be narrow and inward looking. I therefore start with a brief section on my early life and travels, which provided a context for my political beliefs.

Throughout all the ups and downs of political life I have been sustained by Linda, and together we faced the loss of our son. I dedicate this memoir to her.

Chapter 1

Before Europe

I come from a family of West Country textile manufacturers, descended from John Heathcoat, the son of a farmer who in 1808 invented a machine for making lace. He became an MP for Tiverton, sharing the seat with Lord Palmerston, and started the family political tradition.

My father, being the youngest of four brothers, joined the army, so my childhood was one of frequent moves: to Germany, then Egypt, then a succession of postings in England, ending up in Yorkshire. Family life centred on Devon, where my uncle Derry was MP for Tiverton and was Chancellor of the Exchequer under Harold Macmillan. From an early age I absorbed a belief in free trade, internationalism, and the imperative that Britain should maintain her competitiveness in industry and commerce.

After leaving Eton, aged 17, I went for a year to Canada, where I worked for the Hudson's Bay Company, first in Montreal and then at a trading station on the Moose River in Northern Ontario. After this I went on a lengthy trip across Canada and the United States in an anti-clockwise arc, travelling by Greyhound bus on a '$99 for 99 days' ticket. I had some addresses and contacts but mostly travelled alone with no bookings, relying on finding a cheap hotel on arrival. I have never forgotten the generosity of a black truck-driver in Flagstaff, Arizona, who put me up in his own home when he spotted me late at night, obviously in need of somewhere to stay. I was captivated by the whole North American experience: the energy, the freedom, and the prosperity which seemed to be spread much more widely than at home. Eventually I reached New York

1

and crossed back to England by ship in time to go up to Christ Church, Oxford, in 1967 to start my degree.

I engaged sporadically in the Oxford Union, and became president of the Oxford University Conservative Association, a large and competitive organization known for its imaginative electoral practices. The late 1960s were a time of political turmoil, with giant demonstrations in Grosvenor Square against the Vietnam War, student sit-ins and left-wing factionalism, as disillusionment with the Labour government set in. There was increasing alarm about Britain's economic performance, as successive industries were ravaged by foreign competition and our industrial relations became ever worse. My only sporting achievement during those three years was to box for the university.

After leaving Oxford in 1970, I resolved to see as much of the world as possible before starting in business, so set off to explore South America, then in stages crossed the Pacific to New Zealand, arriving in Australia in time for Christmas. In the New Year I moved on to Singapore, where the Commonwealth Heads of Government Conference was starting, and I managed to get accredited as a reporter for the event. In a world less traumatized by terrorism access was easier then. The Conference issued the Singapore Declaration of Principles which re-established the Commonwealth as a 'voluntary association of independent sovereign states', which would cooperate in the pursuit of peace, self-determination, free trade, equal rights and the elimination of poverty. This seemed to me to be an admirable definition of international cooperation but Ted Heath, who led for the British government, was already negotiating to join the European Economic Community, with a different destination in mind.

Using the same credentials as a newspaper correspondent I next went to South Vietnam, where the Americans still had 300,000 troops. They had already lost 50,000 dead, and the political situation was serious, as the South Vietnamese government lacked the political strength to be a reliable foundation for the American military effort. I visited a number of combat bases around Hué and

Da Nang, and witnessed an extraordinary act of bravery by an American GI who threw himself on a grenade which had been lobbed over the perimeter fence and had landed amongst us. By chance the Chinese fuse failed to detonate and he was not killed, but I wrote a testimonial recording the incident, and R.B. Helle of the 5th Marines was subsequently awarded a Navy Cross for his action.

I continued northwards to Hong Kong, and then across to Cambodia, Thailand, India, Nepal and finally Iran, where the rule of the Shah seemed unshakeable, a judgement shared by all foreign policy experts until the Islamic Revolution reached his gates. I was now near the end of my journey, low on funds and with a looming date with an employer in London. There was no political purpose to my travels, but certain ideas had started to ferment; in particular the significance of global competition, the emerging dynamism of new markets, and a belief in the nation state as the essential unit of self-government.

I arrived back in London in 1971 to what seemed a grey and dis-contented England, where Ted Heath's government and the trade unions were limbering up for future battles. A mood of national resignation had set in, together with a loss of self-confidence, and this influenced the debate on whether Britain should join the EEC, or Common Market as it was still called. This question had hung over British politics since the end of the Second World War, when the government had rejected membership of any exclusively European body for fear of compromising American leadership of the West or undermining our trade links with the Commonwealth. This had changed in 1963, when Harold Macmillan applied for member-ship of the EEC but was vetoed by General de Gaulle on the grounds that Britain did not have a European vocation and was too attached to the United States, from whom we were buying Polaris nuclear missiles. Four years later, a Labour government under Harold Wilson applied to join, and was again vetoed by de Gaulle.

By now it was obvious that Britain was no longer an industrial powerhouse, and Commonwealth trade was in comparative decline, so it was attractive to get inside the comforting tariff wall of the

Common Market. With de Gaulle out of office, and the more emollient Georges Pompidou installed as President of France, Ted Heath successfully negotiated new terms of entry. No one could doubt Heath's personal commitment, or his attention to detail: the magazine *Private Eye* satirized Heath as 'The Grocer' – a reference to his extraordinary knowledge of negotiations about the price of vegetables. I thought that the EEC would be the instrument of modernization and renewal, opposed only by a strange alliance of the romantic right and the Labour left. When later that year Parliament voted to join, I opened a bottle of champagne.

I qualified as a chartered accountant with Price Waterhouse & Co and then joined British Electric Traction Ltd, an industrial conglomerate with subsidiaries in the film, music, and newspaper industries. Here I saw the twilight of an industrial system plagued by a multitude of small craft unions, each jealously guarding their marked-out territory. For instance, typesetting for newspapers was done on hot metal machines invented a hundred years before. These mechanical marvels had a keyboard by which the operator selected individual letter moulds, into which molten lead was poured from a vat on the same machine to create a line of solid type, which was then assembled on a page, which was sent for preparation to another operative, in another union, for eventual use in printing (by a third union). This was industrial archaeology rather than business, and it needed more than entry to the EEC to change it.

The dominant political question of the 1970s was how to run a productive economy without inflation in the face of uncompromising trade union power. A failure to resolve this defeated the Heath government and eventually drove out the Labour government which replaced it. Many in the Conservative party seemed to accept that government was impossible without a political accommodation with the large trade unions, and that some kind of permanent prices and incomes policy was inevitable. The advent of Margaret Thatcher as Conservative leader in 1975 promised something different and I became a convinced supporter after sitting next to her at a dinner. Not that her arrival heralded many jokes: at the next Conservative fundraising ball she dispensed with the customary light pleasantries in favour of a detailed lecture on the Socialist menace.

I decided to try for Parliament and in 1976 was selected to fight Brent South. The Borough of Brent, like Gaul, was divided into three parts: Brent North was Conservative, represented by the extrovert Rhodes Boyson, who campaigned enthusiastically for corporal punishment in schools. The other two constituencies were solidly Labour – in the case of Brent South, immovably so. My Conservative supporters were mostly marooned in the relatively prosperous wards of Willesden and Wembley. There were two other groups of potential supporters: first, the Gujarati Asians who had been expelled from East Africa and admitted to Britain by the previous Conservative government; and second, the white working-class critics of Labour's uncontrolled immigration policy. These two groups of supporters were best kept apart.

Meanwhile, I had met Linda Adams and we were married a year later, in February 1978. Being an artist, Linda certainly felt there were other things in life more important than politics, but I was nevertheless resolved on a political career. Nationally, the Labour government lurched from one crisis to another and had to be bailed out by an IMF loan. When it lost its overall majority in Parliament it was rescued by the formation of a Lib-Lab Pact, which achieved very little for the Liberal Party and nothing for the country. The industrial chaos of the 1978–9 Winter of Discontent ended the illusion that Labour could somehow manage the trade unions, and a vote of no confidence in the House of Commons finally triggered a general election on 3 May 1979.

My Labour opponent was Laurie Pavitt, a kindly deaf pacifist. Behind him was a formidable trade union machine for getting out the Labour vote, and a Labour-controlled Brent council which knew how to do favours for the very large immigrant population, the second largest in London after Southall. Arrayed against that, I had a very part-time agent, Mike Ryan, who had been a journalist in Ireland and whose wife ran a boarding house for itinerant workers.

5

Friends came out by day to help before returning to what they called London in the evening. We tramped the streets, leafleted the shopping centres and toured the constituency in an open double-decker bus fitted with a loudhailer, which played a terrible tune called 'Maggie's March' by the True Blues. The candidates' public meeting was a lively event as the National Front and the Workers' Revolutionary Party both fielded candidates. I lost, by 11,616 votes, but nationally the Conservative party was the outright winner. It was soon clear that the government, or at least the Prime Minister, was set on a far-reaching reform of every aspect of public life.

Keith Joseph, unfairly lampooned as the 'mad monk', came to speak to the Coningsby Club, a dining group of Oxford and Cambridge graduates that I was chairman of. He rejected the search for the 'middle ground', which he described as a compromise between politicians, based on electoral expediency, and unrelated to the aspirations of the people. Instead he looked for ideas which could be shared with the electorate, and even political opponents, which he called the 'common ground' and could be used to reverse the country's decline. I wanted to be part of this battle of ideas, but the next election was at least four years away. By now I was assistant finance director of the British Technology Group, which had been formed out of the National Enterprise Board, set up by Labour to manage public sector investments in industry. This gave me a good view of the ever-shifting frontier between government and industry, and made me an enthusiast for the government's later privatization programme.

Parliamentary seats started to advertise for candidates and I applied. Retirements and deaths, scandals and resignations, majorities and boundary changes, were all eagerly pored over by the band of hopefuls looking for winnable seats. I was rejected in Gainsborough, shortlisted for Stratford-upon-Avon, runner-up in Perth and narrowly missed Richmond. Then Wells came up, where I had a reasonably strong claim because of my West Country connections, and I won on the first ballot. The following month, Mrs Thatcher called a general election against a Labour Party led by

Michael Foot, whose trademark walking cane was looking increasingly like a white stick. The 1983 result was shattering for Labour: they were nearly overtaken in votes by the newly formed SDP-Liberal Alliance party. The Conservative majority was 144, including the newly elected member for Wells.

Chapter 2

Parliament

I loved the House of Commons right from the start. It combined the camaraderie of belonging to a political party with the friction and rivalry of a competitive system. There was then no induction or guidance for new MPs, nor any maps of the Palace of Westminster, so the discovery of new corridors, rooms and bars went on for some years. The first thing I needed was an office, a process in theory controlled by the whips, but reckoning occupation is nine-tenths of the law Michael Howard and I scanned the list of those moving on, or up, or out, and secured for ourselves a reasonably large office to share, which even had a window.

MPs have to be general practitioners in their constituencies, but the House of Commons requires specialization and I went for trade, industry, farming and energy policy. I stood for the secretaryship of the Conservative Energy Committee, and even this lowly position was contested. I won against Edwina Currie, generally regarded as the most pushy of the new intake.

Quite soon, Europe started to intrude on all of these issues, in ways that had not been predicted when we joined the EEC. I was struck by how many of the laws and regulations we were passing had their origin in Brussels, and seemed to go through without much scrutiny. The House of Commons was adorned by pictures and murals illustrating the various struggles to achieve self-government and representative democracy, and I wondered if we were being true to that tradition. It was central to the constitution that taxation and expenditure should be under parliamentary control, and this principle was tested within a few months of the election.

Although it was always known that Britain would make a substantial contribution to the Community budget, it was not clear why this should be increasing so fast, particularly against a background of spending cuts at home. The budget was already under fire for its waste and mismanagement, but the House was now being asked to approve a further increase, and to make our contributions automatic. Geoffrey Howe, the Foreign Secretary, had to explain all this, and his assurances were to become wearily familiar and always disappointed: 'There is agreement that the Community's budgetary arrangements must be reformed, that spending must be brought under control ... On budgetary reform there has been a sea change in thinking in the Community ...' I did not support the government in the vote which ended the debate, a gesture of disobedience which was hardly heroic but was noted by the whips, who held the key to all advancement.

I spoke again in the next European debate: 'In Westminster Budgets, taxes are often increased and, in subsequent years, reduced. What we are being asked to do here, however, is to transfer permanently an additional part of our revenue to an extra-parliamentary, extra-national body. That is the constitutional question that affects the historic duties and powers of the Parliament to which I have been elected.' By now I belonged to the Conservative European Reform Group, a small backbench group with a fluctuating and imprecise membership, led by Jonathan Aitken, Teddy Taylor, and Sir Hugh Fraser, whose hawklike presence and rolling oratory, replete with classical and biblical allusions, enlivened these debates. Before this, the job of criticizing the EEC was carried on mostly by isolated individuals, so the CERG has a claim to be the first organized eurosceptic group, at least in parliamentary terms. Much later, when the flaws in the European project became obvious, the world of euroscepticism expanded remarkably and included all sorts of MPs and ex-ministers who had been silent in the early days. The CERG's immediate concerns in 1984 were assuaged by the achievement of the Prime Minister in demanding and getting a two-thirds reduction in Britain's contribution to the Community Budget, an exercise in handbag diplomacy which was still talked about with awe when I joined the Foreign Office ten years later.

The other subject on which I showed some rebelliousness was defence, and specifically arms control. I kept asking about the cost of the proposed Trident nuclear deterrent, and signed an Early Day Motion asking for the project to be re-appraised and checked against other systems. This was reported in the *Western Daily Press* as, 'West Country MP in Trident revolt', and my Whip, Robert Boscawen MC, strode up to me in the division lobby that evening and said, 'I see Somerset has a new defence policy'. A friend in the whips office, Mark Lennox-Boyd, told me that my appointment as a Parliamentary Private Secretary, the lowest rung on the career ladder, had been put on hold.

Meanwhile, the government was fighting a bitter national strike by the National Union of Mineworkers, whose president, Arthur Scargill, had called the strike without the ballot required by the NUM's own rules. The government eventually won and this, more than any legal reforms, ended the period of unrestrained trade union militancy. The effect was subsequently reinforced when the Murdoch press broke the power of the print unions by moving its operation to Wapping and beating the consequential strike.

In the year following the election, the IRA blew up the Grand Hotel in Brighton during the Conservative Party conference, killing five people including the MP Tony Berry. Norman Tebbit was carried out of the rubble on a stretcher and his wife Margaret was permanently paralysed. The Chief Whip, John Wakeham, was badly hurt and his wife, Roberta, was killed. Earlier that year they had both come to Wells when John spoke at our constituency supper club, and I remembered how charming Roberta had been. Despite all this, Leon Brittan, who was Home Secretary, kept his appointment to come and speak to my Wells Association the following weekend, and stayed in our small rented cottage in a wood on the Waldegrave Estate. The local police turned out in force and a sniffer dog from Bristol arrived to check the village hall where the dinner was to be held, and ate part of the first course. A police detachment camped all night in our minute front porch, while we slept soundly within.

The following year I became Parliamentary Private Secretary (PPS) to Norman Lamont, who was a defence minister under the Secretary of State, Michael Heseltine. Norman quite often got into scrapes of one sort or another. He was responsible for defence procurement and our first visit was to Rosyth Dockyard in Fife, which occasioned a near riot. Rosyth was run by the Royal Navy, but there were plans to contract it out to industrial bidders and this was furiously opposed by the trade unions and workforce, who surrounded the building we were in and barricaded the entrance. The Navy showed no aptitude for industrial warfare, as we ran in confusion from one end of the building to the other, ducking under windows and eventually bolting out through the kitchen.

Rather more serious was the Westland affair, in which a small helicopter company nearly brought down the government. Previous disputes in the cabinet had mostly been about the pace of reform, with the 'wets' urging caution and the 'drys' wanting action. This time, Europe was to intrude – a harbinger of future battles. Westland Helicopters was based in Yeovil, very near to my constituency, and it had become clear that it would not survive without linking up to a larger concern. What should have been a piece of routine industrial restructuring became a trial of strength within government as Michael Heseltine was determined, from his desk in the Ministry of Defence, to create a European solution in opposition to the projected link with Sikorski of America. As a PPS in the department, I could see the pressure building as Michael Heseltine tried to assemble a European helicopter consortium to take over Westland, but this did not have the support of the Westland board or his cabinet colleagues. From being a disagreement within government it boiled over into a very public row, when Michael stormed out of a cabinet meeting and resigned. He presented the matter publicly as Europe versus America, but it was more about whether a cabinet minister should run a one-man industrial policy. Leon Brittan, who had to resign over the leaking of a ministerial letter by his Trade and Industry department, was strongly pro-European but opposed the Heseltine plan. The government survived the Westland storm but it was the first major challenge to the authority of the Prime Minister. Her critics waited for their next opportunity, and Michael Heseltine embarked on a speaking tour of Conservative constituencies, including mine.

Britain's prospects were transformed in these years but the idea that the Thatcher government's achievements were in any way inevitable is disproved by the record of rebellions, bloodied ministers, and by-election defeats. The House was often in uproar, and frequently sat very late: for instance, the bill to abolish the Greater London Council was debated through a day, the next night and the following day, without a break. But by late 1986 the government had regained the initiative. Neil Kinnock was trying to peddle an unsaleable Labour defence policy, the privatization programme was working, the sale of council houses to sitting tenants was popular, the economy was improving and unemployment was falling. Norman Lamont had moved to the Treasury, where I as his PPS attended the morning conferences, and I gave one piece of advice which turned out to be prophetic: the Treasury should not agree to abolish domestic rates as a source of revenue and replace them with the Community Charge (later dubbed the Poll Tax), which would be much harder to collect. I knew that Nigel Lawson, as Chancellor, had his own doubts but he was not pushing them to the point of insistence. The 1987 Conservative election manifesto contained, near the end, a one sentence commitment to bring in the Community Charge to pay for local government, a promise that was to have regime changing consequences.

The general election was called for 11 June and the Conservative lead was never seriously under threat. Candidates in elections fight a ground war and are curiously detached from the air war going on at national level. Margaret Thatcher's later account describes arguments, wobbles and rogue polls, but on the streets the campaign always felt right and in the event it was another triumph, a third win. There was a small swing to Labour but the government's majority was 102. The SDP-Liberal Alliance, led by the Davids, Owen and Steel, lost ground and this helped me in Wells where I increased my majority over Alan Butt Philip, an angular old Etonian who was standing for the fifth time.

Chapter 3

Government

In the new Parliament, Douglas Hurd as Home Secretary asked me to be his PPS. My job was to be a kind of parliamentary scout, to keep in touch with backbench opinion and pull the minister out of holes. I was given good access to the department and could participate in most of the discussions, which ranged from prevention of terrorism to immigration, gun control, prisons, war crimes, official secrets and broadcasting. But it was not like being a minister and I was glad when I joined the government the following year, through election to the whips office. Whips are the floor managers of parliamentary proceedings, making sure that bills are presented, ministers turn up, committees are manned, and the government gets its business through. They are also the party disciplinarians, appealing to loyalty or reason, or occasionally by applying the black arts of cajolery or threat, although these are best used sparingly. I was the West Country whip, and also attached to the Department of Energy, where Cecil Parkinson was legislating to privatize the electricity supply industry. His opposite number was one Tony Blair, already tactically adroit, and shameless in making public use of material that had been supplied in confidence to the trade unions as part of the consultation process. He unwisely pledged to take the industry back into public ownership, but that was soon abandoned.

Whips shared everything, supported each other and were always on duty. It was probably the only really loyal organization in politics. But mistakes did happen. One evening I was nominated as a teller in a division of the House, after having dined with Ian Gow, an amusing and original colleague who was killed the following year by the Provisional IRA, who planted a bomb under his car at home. The job of tellers is to count MPs as they leave the aye or no lobbies and report the numbers to the Speaker, who then announces the result. Having perhaps sampled Ian Gow's hospitality too freely, I undercounted by 10 the number of Labour MPs leaving the no lobby and the discrepancy was spotted next day, as the total number of names recorded as having voted did not tally with the number I had reported. This could have meant a public announcement on the floor of the House, but Labour's enthusiasm for this disappeared when I pointed out that the Labour teller, whose job it was to scrutinize my counting, had therefore made the same mistake. In the event the matter was dealt with by a discreet amendment to the record, but I stopped dining with Ian Gow, at least before counting the votes.

After I had been in the whips office a little over a year, there was an unplanned government reshuffle when Nigel Lawson resigned as Chancellor of the Exchequer. Tension between him and the Prime Minister had been rising for some time over the question of whether Britain should join the Exchange Rate Mechanism (ERM), whereby member states agreed to keep the value of their currencies stable against each other. Nigel Lawson saw this as a valuable way of fighting inflation by imposing an external discipline on the British economy, but the Prime Minister was doubtful of any attempt to 'buck the market' and, advised by Alan Walters, her economics guru, feared the loss of control over monetary policy. She was also aware that the rest of Europe saw the ERM as a precursor to full monetary union, and she was perceptive about the political implications of this. In June 1988, David Owen asked her in the House to support the idea of a European central bank. She replied, 'We can have a European central bank only when there is a united states of Europe under one sovereign government, and when all the countries have the same economic policy'. Twenty years later, when it was too late, Europe was to learn the truth of this observation.

The Prime Minister was incensed when she discovered that Nigel Lawson had been pursuing an unannounced policy of shadowing the deutschmark, as an alternative to joining the ERM. This policy had damaging consequences as it prevented the Chancellor putting up interest rates to damp down an overheating domestic economy. Matters came to a head in June 1989, just before a European Summit in Madrid, when Nigel Lawson as Chancellor, and Geoffrey Howe as Foreign Secretary, formed up to her and demanded that a date be set for British entry to the ERM. The Prime Minister refused, and maintained this position at Madrid, but in order to stop her two most senior ministers resigning she had to give ground, so she agreed that we might eventually join, if certain conditions were met. At this point the government entered a long glide path to disaster.

The next month, the Prime Minister moved Geoffrey Howe, protesting, from the Foreign Office, but this was far from the end of the matter. Relations with Nigel Lawson deteriorated further and when the Prime Minister refused to sack her advisor, Alan Walters, Lawson resigned and was replaced by John Major. This meant a number of consequential changes, and the next morning at home I was telephoned by Mrs Thatcher offering me the job of Parliamentary Under Secretary at the Department of the Environment, replacing Virginia Bottomley, who went to Health. When I first got into the House, Margaret Thatcher had a slightly disconcerting habit of calling me 'Derry', confusing me with my uncle Derry who had been Chancellor of the Exchequer when Margaret entered the House in 1959. I eventually corrected her, and she then stopped calling me anything at all until she rang to offer me this job. The next day, a Saturday, the post office delivered to my constituency home near Wells three large red boxes in their locked canvas bags, containing everything that a junior minister should know about a new department.

The Department of the Environment was in Marsham Street and was, by common agreement, the ugliest building in Westminster, and the least environmental, and was eventually demolished. But it was a good department to join as the subject matter was easy to grasp and there was a lot happening. There appeared on my desk a 275-page paperback, the Environmental Protection Bill, which had been in preparation for years and was shortly to have its First

Reading in the House of Commons. David Trippier, the senior minister for the countryside, and I were to take it through the Commons in the New Year. It was an omnibus bill, covering air pollution, water quality, derelict land, litter, wildlife, recycling, and genetically modified organisms. The unexpected subject of dogs was to cause the biggest problem.

Meanwhile, I decided to try to get out of the office every Friday to visit the real environment. The first excursion was to see from the air the devastation wrought by the great storm of 1987, which had done much damage in southern England. It was thought to be the strongest tempest to hit the country since the famous storm of 1703, written up by Daniel Defoe, which sank 13 Royal Navy ships in the Channel and killed the Bishop of Bath and Wells and his wife in bed, hit by a falling chimney. This time, the main damage was more prosaically limited to trees, millions of which were uprooted and could be seen aligned in recumbent swathes through the forested parts of Sussex and Kent. There was little a visiting minister could do, but it did spur a change in forestry policy towards better planting of more species.

The Secretary of State, Chris Patten, planned a White Paper, disapproved of by his predecessor Nick Ridley, to bring together the government's environmental policies and point a way forward. The result, titled This Common Inheritance, has aged quite well. It set out an ambitious programme, but candidly faced up to the cost of environmental policies and the trade-off between some environmental goals and economic growth and welfare. On global warming, it was the first to commit the government to a programme of carbon emission reductions through energy efficiency, particularly in buildings and transport, forestry, and changes in power generation. Nuclear power had a chapter of its own and was accepted as a good way of generating electricity without emitting carbon. The science of global warming was recognized as being provisional, with many uncertainties. It was only later that the theory became more like an ideology, immune to contrary evidence.

18

The green lobby was gathering force, and in the previous year's European Parliament elections the Green Party got more than twice as many votes as the Liberal Democrats. Their campaign methods could be equally unscrupulous and sometimes had perverse results. For instance, the privatization of the water industry had made water quality a hot topic, and it fell to me to oversee the sale of shares in the ten regional water companies. The Greens attacked the privatization and ran a series of newspaper advertisements under the heading, 'These are the poisons coming out of your tap', listing chemicals and residues sometimes found in minute quantities in drinking water. This failed to derail the share flotation, but it did give a big boost to the bottled water industry. Bottled water costs 2,000 times as much as tap water and has to be put into bottles made from oil, which are then imported and transported, and eventually the bottles are thrown away. Not very environmental and not a very bright campaign.

I had a brush with the law over the sale of assets owned by the Greater London Council. The GLC had been abolished three years before and I was responsible for the London Residuary Body which was disposing of the property. I reversed a decision of my predecessor, Virginia Bottomley, to transfer a Gay and Lesbian Centre to the Borough of Islington for £1, and instead required the borough to pay something more like its market value. I was immediately sued by Islington Borough on the grounds that I was discriminating against gays and lesbians, and two Treasury Solicitors came to my office to prepare my defence. I explained that I belonged to the socially liberal wing of the Conservative Party and had no desire to discriminate in that way, but I was determined to sell public assets for what they were worth. It was eventually decided that, although the original decision had been made in the name of the government, it was a fair exercise of ministerial discretion to reverse it, and indeed there was no point in having ministers unless they occasionally disagreed – Islington dropped the case before it reached court.

My first experience of European government was to attend the Council of Ministers in Brussels to negotiate various environmental directives. The technical work was done by the European Commission and officials from each of the 12 member states, and ministers then met to settle any outstanding points. The final product, when agreed, was compulsory for 360 million EC citizens, so we were a formidable legislature, and the degree of democratic oversight was minimal. The European Parliament had a say, but was always on the side of more lawmaking at European level. It was all very private and technical, and I could see that being above nations also meant being above democracy.

By contrast, the Environmental Protection Bill inched its way through committee, clause by clause, and eventually returned to the floor of the House for its Report Stage, when important amendments are voted on. By now there was a national campaign running for the compulsory registration of all dogs, which was supposed to cure every problem, including stray dogs, unwanted dogs, sheep worrying and attacks by dangerous dogs. I was against this because it would be expensive to administer and, while responsible owners would pay the necessary fee, the problems were caused by irresponsible owners who would avoid registering. A better solution was to enforce the existing requirement for every dog in a public place to wear a collar and tag, so that the owners could be traced without the need for a central computer with millions of names on it.

The RSPCA, rich and politically well connected, led the campaign for registration, which they doubtless hoped to run themselves. Only the smaller Kennel Club was opposed, and in the dog world size counts. Janet Fookes, MP for Plymouth Drake, had chaired the RSPCA and organized a public meeting of its members and supporters at which I explained my opposition. I was quite shocked to be loudly booed, and when the redoubtable Dame Janet reprimanded them for this, they growled instead. Attention then shifted to the House of Commons where Janet Fookes tabled an amendment to the bill, with support from all parties, requiring a national dog

20

registration scheme. The whips could not predict the outcome, despite our nominal majority of over a hundred.

The debate started after 10.00pm, but the House was full and there was something of a festive atmosphere. The veteran MP Julian Amery (no relation) wondered if dog registration was a way of widening the franchise: 'And why not? In Africa it is perfectly normal for uneducated tribesmen to put their hand or thumb on the ballot paper, so why should not the doggies be allowed to put their paws there? ... There are young men in my constituency who will have the vote next year, who are less competent than some of our canine friends in forming a serious estimate about what should and should not be done.'

Just after midnight I rose to wind up the debate, deploying the case against central registration and answering the points raised in the debate. Then the division was called and we won, by 12 votes. But it was not the end of the matter. The Environmental Protection Bill then went to the House of Lords which voted to insert a dog registration scheme into the bill. The RSPCA's campaign had reached a crescendo, with full page advertisements showing piles of dead dogs, supposedly the consequence of not having a registration scheme. The Department was all for giving in, perhaps by allowing a pilot scheme of some kind, but I was determined to oppose it. To my great relief we received a message from the Prime Minister that what was wrong before was still wrong, and the Lords amendment must be rejected. This time the debate was more sombre and the mood more determined. I had an extra argument to deploy, from Northern Ireland, which had run a dog registration scheme for seven years and it was estimated that less then half of all dogs there were registered. I spoke twice in the debate and at ten o'clock the House divided. We won by 3 votes. It was a small victory in the great scheme of things but I am sure it spared us an expensive and unworkable piece of bureaucracy. I noticed that some of the journalists who supported a dog registration scheme were the same people who complained at other times about over-regulation.

One argument I was not allowed to deploy against dog registration was to point to the increasingly fruitless efforts to register everyone for the Community Charge. This flat rate tax, to be paid by everyone, was held to be superior to the domestic rates, or property tax, which was only paid by heads of household and therefore created a 'free rider' problem. The Community Charge was invented by Victor Rothschild and had great theoretical advantages as a way of paying for local government. But good theories don't always make good government, and in practice it broke the four 'maxims of taxation' laid down by Adam Smith in the *Wealth of Nations* in 1776, summarized as, Equity, Certainty, Convenience and Efficiency.

I had been a vocal critic of this proposed tax, but on joining the government I had to accept collective responsibility. I did have an argument with Mrs Thatcher about it at a club dinner in 1988. Parliament is full of dining clubs and I joined a number: the One Nation, the Progress Trust, No Turning Back, the Burke Club, the Third Term Group and one or two smaller ones. Some of these groups had a right or left flavour; others were just an agreeable place to discuss policy and gossip. The Prime Minister was generous with her time in attending such dinners, and at one of them, called the No. 5 Group, there was a vigorous discussion about the impending Community Charge and I thought I had gone too far in the way I attacked it. But she seemed to enjoy being challenged and no offence was taken, although it was clear that nothing would deflect her from the new tax. That sense of purpose she brought to everything she did, so invigorating for those who served under her, so important for national renewal, was now to cause her downfall.

The Community Charge, or Poll Tax as it became known, was introduced in England and Wales in 1990. Scotland had got it the year before, which caused further resentment as they claimed they were being used as a guinea pig. It became a nightmare to implement. Houses are easy to count and tax, but people are more elusive. Local authorities used the transition to hike up their expenditure, so the individual charge was much higher than planned, but people blamed the government, not the local authorities. Refuseniks announced they would not pay. There were riots in Trafalgar Square. The trouble about tax is precisely that everyone pays it, so rows about tax tend to be big ones: it was how we lost the American colonies.

The Department of the Environment bore the brunt of this, and there were so many letters to answer from angry MPs and the public that we shared out the correspondence to relieve the burden on the ministers most affected, Michael Portillo and Chris Chope. New reliefs and exemptions were brought in to blunt the criticisms of unfairness, and the cost to the Treasury soared, but still the opposition mounted. All this took its toll on the popularity of the government, which was now trailing in the polls, and also on the standing of the Prime Minister. But it was the European issue that triggered her removal.

Margaret Thatcher sometimes called herself a European idealist, but these ideals differed from those of her foreign secretaries, and even more from those who ran the European Union. Her success in renegotiating Britain's unfair EU budget contribution encouraged her to think that with force and verve she could have the same effect in Europe as at home in changing attitudes and protecting national interests. She was enthusiastic for the Single Market programme, which she saw as a way of completing the original aim of a Common Market in goods and services. But that was about it. In her memoirs, Mrs Thatcher described how she was slow to realize how relentless was the underlying movement towards political union, and in her third term she resolved to fight it:

Isolated I might be in the European Community – but taking the wider perspective, the federalists were the real isolationists, clinging grimly to a half-Europe when Europe as a whole was being liberated; toying with protectionism when truly global markets were emerging; obsessed with schemes of centralisation when the greatest attempt at centralisation – the Soviet Union – was on the point of collapse.

23

She tried and failed to dislodge the Franco-German axis that was the motor of EU integration, and one of her initiatives, to encourage French misgivings about German reunification, was a mistake. She also found that the Italians were hopeless allies in any attempt to construct a different line of influence. She occasionally made common cause with the Dutch over budgetary discipline, or the Danes over monetary union, but she dismissed most small countries as far too willing to agree to anything which gave them influence at the top table and subsidies to spend at home.

The European ideal was to be achieved by monetary union, and this was laid out in the Delors Plan of 1989. Jacques Delors was the longest serving President of the European Commission, experienced, wily and determined. As a French Socialist and a frequent critic of 'Anglo Saxon values', he and Margaret Thatcher were never destined to be friends, but they had a wary respect for each other. Delors was also flattering about British diplomacy and told me that if the European Commission was able to recruit purely on merit, it would be run mostly by French and British officials.

What exasperated Mrs Thatcher was how Delors, whom she regarded as an unelected civil servant, had become, in her words, 'a fully fledged political spokesman for federalism'. In July 1988, Delors told the European Parliament that within ten years he expected 80 per cent of economic and social legislation would be made by the European Community. He followed this up by addressing the TUC Conference in Bournemouth where he told delegates that collective bargaining should be conducted at European level, and that the single market would be overlain by a 'social Europe' of regulations and protected rights. He invited his audience to 'join the architects of Europe'. This was a shrewd appeal to the Labour Party which had abandoned its outright hostility to the EC but was still trying to come to terms with market disciplines and globalization. The Delors formula offered a free market within a controlled 'European social and economic space', and this shifted the party towards support for European integration, which was later to be a key ingredient in New Labour.

24

The same month, October 1988, Margaret Thatcher responded to these provocations in a landmark speech in Bruges. Preparations for a major speech on Europe by the Prime Minister had been going on for some months and it was originally intended to focus on economic issues, where her general support for the single market programme might prevent her stepping on too many mines. Nervous Foreign Office officials watched as successive drafts moved on to ever more controversial territory. The speech started by outlining Britain's commitment to Europe over many centuries – 'our destiny is in Europe, as part of the Community'. With that out of the way she then set off in a different direction, starting with the point that, 'The European Community is *one* manifestation of that European identity, but it is not the only one'. She went on to describe a number of principles for constructing an open, enterprising Europe which included a strong Atlantic alliance and needed no more treaties. 'Willing and active cooperation between independent sovereign states is the best way to build a successful Economic Community'. Then she issued an explicit challenge to the prophets of integration which obviously had Jacques Delors in the cross-wires:

> Working together more closely does not require power to be centralised in Brussels or decisions to be taken by an appointed bureaucracy. Indeed it is ironic that just when those countries such as the Soviet Union, which have tried to run everything from the centre, are learning that success depends on dispersing power and decisions away from the centre, there are some in the Community who seem to want to move in the opposite direction.
>
> We have not successfully rolled back the frontiers of the state in Britain, only to see them re-imposed at a European level with a European super-state exercising a new dominance from Brussels.

The Bruges speech caused an immense furore. It was not part of polite European diplomacy to have one of its members directly challenge the assumptions on which EC construction rested. But

Margaret Thatcher was always more of a warrior than diplomat. At home, Geoffrey Howe, the Foreign Secretary, registered quiet disapproval and he later wrote, 'I can now see that this was probably the moment in which there began to crystallise the conflict of loyalty with which I was to struggle for perhaps too long.'

The following year, the Delors Plan on monetary union was published, advocating a three-stage approach to a single European currency. German doubts about giving up the fabled strength and stability of the deutschmark were no match for French determination to end the dominance of the Bundesbank. From a British and German perspective, monetary union meant giving up control over money and interest rates; from the French point of view it meant regaining control over matters which they had already ceded to Germany. The creation of a single European currency became a key aim of French foreign policy.

Mrs Thatcher was against any such proposal, and suspicious of any moves in that direction, including the idea that Britain should join the ERM. This had been refined into a scheme of managed exchange rates, whereby participating EU countries would fix their exchange rates together but allow a degree of fluctuation; sometimes called the semi-pegged system. The Prime Minister had already lost Nigel Lawson over this, and had been forced to give some ground, but she still believed that markets decide exchange rates, not politicians. She was therefore dismayed when John Major, Nigel Lawson's successor as Chancellor, also saw entry to the ERM as necessary to give credibility to the government's counter-inflation strategy. The Prime Minister's authority was now weakening and, having already lost a Chancellor and Foreign Secretary over Europe, she could hold out no longer. Outnumbered in the cabinet, and with the CBI, the trade unions, the opposition parties, and most of the press in favour of joining, Mrs Thatcher conceded, and Britain entered the ERM in October 1990. She later wrote, 'Nothing is more obstinate than a fashionable consensus'.

This only made her more determined to resist any other moves towards political or monetary union. At the Rome Summit later the same month the Prime Minister fought the proposal to set a target date for the next stage of monetary union, but was outvoted 11 to 1. In her follow-up statement in the House of Commons she asserted, 'We would not be prepared to have a single currency imposed on us, nor to surrender the use of the pound sterling as our currency . . . What is the point of trying to get elected to parliament only to hand over sterling and the powers of this House to Europe?' She then gave her famous triple no: 'The President of the Commission, Mr Delors, said at a press conference the other day that he wanted the European Parliament to be the democratic body of the Community, he wanted the Commission to be the Executive and he wanted the Council of Ministers to be the Senate. No. No. No.'

This went down very well on the Conservative back benches, but two days later Geoffrey Howe resigned from the Cabinet. On being removed as Foreign Secretary, he had accepted the consolation prize of Leader of the House but his personal relationship with the Prime Minister had become even worse, and they were barely on speaking terms. We crowded into the chamber to hear his resignation speech and listened with amazement as this soft-spoken man gave vent to years of frustration and made a highly personal attack on the Prime Minister's entire European strategy and motives. She later described it as 'this final act of bile and treachery'. The next day, Michael Heseltine announced he was challenging her for leadership of the Conservative Party.

I felt despair as events unfolded but I sent a message to Peter Morrison, the Prime Minister's campaign manager, that I would certainly be voting for her. MPs are a sophisticated and duplicitous electorate and it is not unknown for the same MP to appear as a committed supporter in the yes column of each campaign team. The result of the first ballot was certainly worse than expected: she won, but was four votes short of the 15 per cent majority required to prevent a second round. This was conveyed to the Prime Minister in Paris, where she was attending a security summit with the presidents of the United States and Russia, and she then had to sit through a banquet at Versailles while her future was being decided at home. The question was, should she stand in the next round, or could another candidate, perhaps John Major, stop a Heseltine win? There were fevered discussions, and the next day she saw the Cabinet, one by one; the message was, yes, they would support her if she stood but no, she couldn't win. The mood gathering on the back benches was that with the Prime Minister we would have the poll tax, and with the poll tax we would lose the next election.

I was dining with the No Turning Back Group that evening, a little way from the House of Commons, and as we debated we saw microphones and TV cameras pressed to the window. Peter Lilley, newly in the cabinet, repeated his view that the Prime Minister could not win, but the majority of us sent a message of support that she should fight on, conveyed to her in person late that night. But the next day she resigned. The greatest Prime Minister since Churchill had been defeated, not by the electorate, but by her own party.

That afternoon the House was full for a debate on a Motion of No Confidence, tabled by the Opposition. Neil Kinnock misjudged the mood with a sour speech, claiming credit for the Prime Minister's fall. I listened to her reply with sadness and fascination. She was not particularly eloquent, but there was something heroic about the way she set out her beliefs for the last time and dealt with all interventions. Maybe her certainties and sense of mission had now become infected with intolerance, but at her best she was magnificent.

John Major and Douglas Hurd entered the lists and I supported Douglas. I knew him well, admired the way he concentrated on the important things, and although of course I disagreed with him about Europe, this was declared, and I thought this was better than the managerial route to the same end which I detected in John Major. Douglas was never going to win, and he was not known as the careerist's candidate, but the result was not humiliating: John Major, 185; Michael Heseltine, 131; Douglas Hurd 56. We were thus spared a Heseltine premiership. His leadership and oratorical gifts would have ensured a brilliant trajectory but we would all have been hit by the falling debris, and he would probably have taken Britain into the euro, with disastrous consequences. Leadership is important but it has to be in the right direction. John Major formed a new government, with Michael Heseltine brought in as Secretary of State for the Environment, with instructions to fix the Community Charge. I never met my new boss in the department; instead I was telephoned two days later by the Prime Minister, when I was just about to answer an environment debate in the House, saying I was to leave Environment, and offering me an equivalent post in the Department of Energy. No reason for this switch was given, but some years later when I asked Michael Heseltine he said I was not interventionist enough for him.

The Department of Energy was small, with only two junior ministers, Colin Moynihan, who did oil and gas and renewables, and me doing coal, nuclear power and electricity. The Secretary of State, John Wakeham, was working on the public flotation of the electricity industry and I liked the slightly mischievous way he dealt with the problems. He was also much involved in broader government business, so he gave Colin and me considerable latitude in the department, provided we caused no strikes.

I pushed energy efficiency as hard as I could, as it made sense at every level, environmental and economic, and the public sector was particularly bad in the way it used and wasted energy. One only had to fly over England at night to see a blaze of wasted light, illuminating the night sky and washing out the most universal and beautiful of all environments, the starry heavens.

On nuclear power, I did my best but failed to restart a construction programme. The story of nuclear power in Britain was not a happy one. We had an early lead but never found the right reactor design to make a commercial success of it, and instead built a string of prototypes. The French took the brave and correct decision to switch to an American-designed Pressurized Water Reactor (PWR) in the early 1970s and then built a series of them to a standardized design. France became a major exporter of low-carbon electricity and nuclear engineering. Meanwhile Britain struggled on with a confused programme of gas-cooled reactors and finally built a PWR at Sizewell in Suffolk. I went to the topping-out ceremony at Sizewell and made suitably upbeat remarks, but there was to be no successor. Hinkley Point in Somerset should have been the site of the next one, but the programme stalled and Britain was eventually reduced to the status of subcontractor.

Britain had the first Industrial Revolution, powered almost entirely by coal. The industry grew to employ over a million men, often working in very dangerous conditions due to the risk of rock falls or underground explosions caused by methane, or the still more deadly coal dust. By 1990, the market was being opened up to other fuels, particularly gas, and British deep-mined coal was being challenged by cheaper coal from abroad. The coal industry was also a climate change offender because it took solid carbon out of the ground, where it had formed over millions of years, and released it in a few seconds into the atmosphere in the form of CO_2.

The industry still employed 60,000 people but the decline was relentless and, despite the trauma of the national coal strike, most miners were personally realistic about the future of the industry. My job was to encourage modernization and also to try to avoid compulsory redundancies. About 10,000 men were leaving the industry on generous terms each year. I visited three deep mines, the first being Daw Mill near Coventry, which was mining a 15-foot thick coal seam still in use today. The next descent was at Goldthorpe in South Yorkshire, where feelings still ran high because of the coal miners' strike. Before I arrived there was a pithead meeting to decide whether to allow a Tory minister down, but having decided to do so they were entirely welcoming. No one should ever turn down the opportunity to visit a deep mine, though it is not for claustrophobics. It was a harsh environment underground: hot, noisy and cramped, as one knelt on a moving conveyor through low tunnels to the face. There, rotating drums tore at the coal which dropped on to another conveyor, and, after the machines had moved forward, the roof was allowed to collapse behind. The decline in underground mining would continue unabated after Labour took power in 1997.

Taking advantage of the fall of communism, I took a delegation of energy experts and businessmen to Poland in July 1991. The Berlin Wall had come down two years before and in Poland a Solidarity-led government was dealing with a legacy of failure and trying to introduce market reforms. It was a fairly chaotic visit, but the contacts led to some further business and it showed beyond doubt how a centrally planned economy wasted energy on a colossal scale.

Our hosts showed us round Warsaw, including the dreadful Palace of Culture, given by Stalin to the people of Poland in 1955, when it was the tallest building in Europe. Most of the city had been destroyed in the Second World War and it was easy to see why the Poles distrust their neighbours. In 1940, the Soviet secret police massacred the whole Polish Officer Corps in the Katyn Forest. In 1944, Warsaw rose against the occupying Germans but on Stalin's orders the advancing Russians failed to help them and the uprising was crushed. The German army then blew up most of what re-mained of Warsaw, street by street, and I saw the contemporary film record of this. Any apologists for these two murderous regimes should study Polish history.

At home, the economy was still in recession with unemployment rising, but inflation was now under control and had even dropped below the rate in Germany. Unfortunately the Chancellor, Norman Lamont, could not reduce interest rates faster to stimulate the economy because we were now in the Exchange Rate Mechanism. This was an early indicator that the demands of the ERM could differ from the needs of the domestic economy, a conflict that was to have dire consequences in the next parliament.

At the same time, the EU was drawing up a new treaty, eventually signed at Maastricht. This inoffensive Dutch town was to give its name to a treaty which would split the Conservative Party. The treaty committed EU members to European Monetary Union, in other words a single currency, and the Prime Minister negotiated an opt-out for the UK. He also, at the insistence of Michael Howard, the

Employment Secretary, secured an opt-out from the Social Chapter which would have put up employment costs and undermined labour market flexibility. These concessions were well received, but there was plenty more in the treaty which would cause great trouble when it had to be ratified after the election.

At least the Poll Tax had been abolished, though the cost of replacing it with the Council Tax was a permanent increase of 2½ per cent on the rate of VAT. The Prime Minister decided to leave the general election as late as possible to give the economy time to strengthen, and this strategy was helped by an ingenious 1992 budget in which Norman Lamont introduced a 20 per cent income tax rate for the low paid, thus establishing the party's tax cutting credentials without giving too much money away.

I and another junior minister, Stephen Dorrell, were shown a draft of the election manifesto to read and comment on. I thought it too long and rather unfocused but not many people read manifestos anyway. More important was the highly successful poster campaign invented by the advertising chief Maurice Saatchi, which featured a 'Labour Tax Bombshell' of £1,250 per household. Parliament was dissolved on 16 March 1992 and I happened to be the last MP to speak, replying to a debate on nuclear power. I finished by quoting the gladiator's oath: 'A new House of Commons will meet in six weeks time, and I fully intend to be here, but exactly who returns and on what side we sit will be decided, as should be, by the electorate. I have no epitaph for this Parliament beyond saying, after Suetonius, "*Ave, Populus, morituri te salutant*" [Hail, People, those who are about to die salute you].'

At the start of the election campaign we were still 3 per cent behind in the polls, but there was always something implausible about Neil Kinnock as prime minister, and during the campaign he did much to reinforce this. John Major held his nerve and his dogged persistence turned the tide. The result was a personal victory: a reduced majority, down to 21, but he had secured for the party a fourth conservative term. It was this result which finally persuaded the Labour Party that the game was up with Socialism and that they had to try something more in tune with people's aspirations. John Major was therefore responsible for the transformation of the left in Britain, which was good for the country even though it would lead to his own defeat.

In Wells, I was home with a slightly reduced majority of 6,649. As we gathered in the House of Commons, mildly surprised still to be in government, thoughts turned to the future. My last red box from the Department of Energy had a rather valedictory tone to it. Colin Moynihan, my co-minister, had lost his seat. John Wakeham had stood down and was going to the House of Lords as Leader. I was still a minister, but in a department that had been abolished. Was I the last defender, or the first casualty, or what?

Chapter 4

New Departments

As John Major started to form his new government, I got a call from Richard Ryder, the Chief Whip, asking me to be Deputy Chief Whip, and I accepted straight away. I liked Richard and I knew that although the job of Deputy was essentially an organizational one, it did give a broad view of what was happening across government and the party generally. I had an office in 12 Downing Street and I set about allocating jobs, offices and committee places to back-benchers. Several new members had to be persuaded that their route to the top lay via the Statutory Instruments Committee.

The Deputy Chief Whip was also Treasurer of Her Majesty's Household. The deed of appointment said I was, 'to have, hold, exercise and enjoy the said Place, together with all Rights, Profits, Privileges and Advantages thereunto belonging'. These advantages turned out to be few in number, but did include a ride in the procession at the State Opening of Parliament. Normally this takes place in November each year, but the one following the election was on a fine May morning, so we rode in horse-drawn open carriages. I shared mine with the formidable David Lightbown, Comptroller of the Household, whose ample girth gave the carriage a pronounced tilt. As we clattered along the Mall we waved our top hats back at people in the crowd, who perhaps thought we were some obscure branch of foreign royalty.

My only other Household duty was to act as an usher at the royal garden parties held at Buckingham Palace in the summer. My job was to keep ahead of the Queen as she moved down her aisle and to choose people out of the crowd to meet her. The Queen was very professional in not chatting too long before disengaging and moving on to the next group, and at one garden party she got ahead of the ushers and one of them had to grab a couple out of the crowd just in time to meet their sovereign. The Queen asked the couple about their life together and the woman replied, 'I've never met him before in my life, your Majesty!'

When I left the job, the Queen gave me an inscribed wand of office, about the length of a billiard cue, but with no obvious purpose. My real job was to manage the work of the other 12 whips, and try to avoid upsets to the government's business. I had a meeting with the Clerk of the House every day, and with the Speaker every week, and I chaired the security committee meetings which were held jointly with officials from the House of Lords. There were inevitable tensions between the desire for open access for the public and the need to protect Parliament from violent disorder or attack. The British constitution is unusual in guaranteeing the Prime Minister's attendance at Question Time in the House of Commons, at exactly the same time every week; an advantage which Guy Fawkes did not have.

The government was very soon in trouble, and three events in the first year were to damage its authority severely. Two were related to Europe and one was about the coal industry. The economy was not out of recession, indeed unemployment was still rising and the housing market badly needed a boost. The case for interest rate cuts was obvious but this could not be done because of Britain's membership of the Exchange Rate Mechanism. We were anchored to the deutschmark and the German central bank, the Bundesbank, was actually raising interest rates there in order to head off inflation. Just as Nigel Lawson's policy of shadowing the deutschmark in the 1980s had prevented us raising interest rates, so now the ERM was preventing us lowering them. Quite simply, the domestic needs of the economy had to come second to our European commitments, and since it was the Prime Minister who had taken us into the ERM as Chancellor, he would not now contemplate a change of policy.

The market now took over: the deutschmark strengthened further and other currencies, including sterling and the lira, weakened. This threatened the stability of the ERM but the Bundesbank, with its duty to contain inflation in Germany, would not cut its interest rate. Norman Lamont as Chancellor was losing faith in the ERM, but in public he had to assert adamantly that everything would be done to keep sterling within the system. Interest rates were raised again and again, and in September the government borrowed £7 billion to defend sterling. Huge profits were made by speculators like George Soros who could sell pounds to the Bank of England at the official rate and buy them back at a cheaper market rate. This showed up the fallacy that the ERM would somehow protect currencies from the predatory speculations of financiers and city traders. In fact it allowed these traders to make far more money betting against the politicians than they would have made in a competitive market of freely floating currencies.

British interest rates were eventually raised to 15 per cent, and £14.5 billion flowed out of the reserves in trying to defend the official rate. Despite feverish negotiations with other EU governments, the situation became hopeless and on Wednesday, 16 September 1992 – christened Black Wednesday – Norman Lamont came out of the Treasury to announce on the steps that, 'Today has been an extremely difficult and turbulent day', and that British membership of the ERM was 'suspended', which meant it was ended. Economically, it turned out to be White Wednesday because it liberated the UK and led to a long period of stable growth. Politically, it was Black Wednesday: a catastrophe, and the Conservative Party's reputation for economic competence was shattered.

As well as sterling, the Italian lire crashed out of the ERM, followed by other devaluations and withdrawals. The following year, the French and Danish currency rates became unsustainable and the ERM was effectively suspended by greatly widening the permitted fluctuation bands. This should have taught everyone a terrible lesson, but some drew different conclusions. The European Commission published an economic paper attributing the collapse to speculators and illogical market reaction. Its solution was to press ahead with full monetary union. According to this view, the problem of exchange rate instability could be avoided by removing the exchange rates. Turmoil in the currency markets could be ended by abolishing the currencies. Whenever there was a crisis, 'more Europe' was always their solution.

The second of the government's problems was Maastricht. The bill to ratify this treaty was put on hold when Denmark rejected it in a referendum, and it would have been better to respect that decision, but John Major had signed the treaty before the election and he wanted it ratified. He called a meeting to discuss tactics and for some reason we met in the Cobra Room under Downing Street, normally reserved for national emergencies. It turned out to be an appropriate setting, as it was decided to take the risk of having no free votes and driving the bill through the House with the full authority of the Prime Minister. The task was now greatly complicated by the ERM debacle, which had shown the folly of rigid commitments which overrode British interests.

I had considerable sympathy with the critics. From the Departments of Environment and Energy I had often been to Brussels to negotiate regulations and directives and I had seen the ratchet operating, whereby policies transferred to Brussels never came back, even if it was found that EU action was clumsy or inefficient. Only the unelected European Commission could propose new measures or the repeal of old ones, and its mission was always to expand the scope and scale of EU action. There was little public scrutiny and the European Parliament only intervened to increase its own authority, and always voted for a bigger EU budget. There were also hundreds of advisory, management and regulatory committees, operating with only the barest political oversight. All this had to be at the expense of national powers – in our case, the House of Commons. In short, the power to take decisions was increasingly being transferred from people who were elected and could be removed, to people who were not elected and could not be removed.

The central feature of the Maastricht Treaty was a binding plan for full monetary union, although John Major had secured an opt-out for the UK. The treaty also added two new fields of policy cooperation: Foreign and Security policy and Justice and Home Affairs. These were controversial extensions of EU responsibility, but there was a difference: they were to be outside the existing Community institutions and would operate government to government. Each member state could therefore retain its veto and the outcome would not be subject to the European Parliament or European Court of Justice. These two new intergovernmental 'pillars' seemed to point to a new and better way of running the EU, offering cooperation without central control. Cynics predicted that the new structure would not last, and they were right: 15 years later this system of national cooperation was abolished and the policies came under EU control.

The Maastricht Treaty also brought in more majority voting, greatly expanded the aid budget for poorer EU countries, and took the EU into new areas such as education, culture, public health and the environment. It was a one-way pipeline from national parliaments to the EU, and there was no return valve. On the other hand, the British opt-out from monetary union was watertight, and the job-destroying Social Chapter had been avoided. The Treaty had been approved by the House of Commons the previous year, with few Conservative objections. Since then John Major had won an election against the odds and so, despite being torn both ways, I felt that he had a right to implement a treaty he had signed. Having decided that, I confess that I played a full and active part in getting the bill through.

The first vote was on a Paving Motion to restart the bill in November. Labour, despite being in favour of the Treaty, opposed it on the grounds that the Social Chapter should not have been excluded. There was an intense whipping operation to calculate the number of likely Conservative rebels and what concessions might get them on board. I am sure the Prime Minister would have resigned if the motion had been lost, as he had already been damaged by Black Wednesday and a defeat would have destroyed his ability to govern. The vote was won by 3, but that was only the start. As a constitutional bill, the committee stage was taken entirely on the floor of the House, which meant that weeks of debate stretched ahead. The first day opened with one and a half hours of points of order and the first amendment was not voted on until 10.00pm the next night. Thereafter it was guerrilla warfare.

The Maastricht rebels were a rich assortment of high principle and low cunning, patriotism and disloyalty, integrity and vanity. All parties that have been in office for some time accumulate a residue of those with frustrated hopes and disappointed ambitions; but others were acting out of long-standing conviction and a belief that the rights of Parliament came before party. There were about 25 hard-core rebels, but others would abstain or vote with them on some issues. They met each week to table amendments and plan tactics, and these proceedings were leaked to us by an anonymous participant.

The rules of party discipline rapidly broke down. It was a feature of parliamentary life that MPs would sometimes vote against the party whip, but this was governed by certain courtesies and conventions. A dissident MP should give notice, and normally discuss the matter with the minister responsible for the legislation to see if some compromise or accommodation might be possible. I knew the game had changed when I walked out of the whips office into the Members Lobby before a division and saw James Cran, unofficial rebel whip, openly exchanging notes with my Labour opposite number, Don Dixon. In later parliaments Cran showed no interest in the European question, so he exemplified a rebel with a cause but no real principles.

With our parliamentary majority at 18, we were extremely vulnerable, and if the opposition parties combined with our dissidents, we would lose. In fact this happened only once during the committee stage, on a comparatively minor clause, but their collusion wrecked the timetable for the bill. They did this by sometimes voting together, by agreement, to defeat the '10 o'clock motion', which was necessary if the House was to sit late. This meant that we never knew in advance what progress the bill would make. Sometimes we sat very late and I often slept on a makeshift camp bed and then wearily planned the business for the next day. At other times we had to draw stumps early. It was ragged, exhausting, and showed that the government was not in control of its own legislation.

Outside the Westminster goldfish bowl, the government was losing the propaganda war. The Foreign Office case was essentially negative, that the Treaty was not too bad and we were protected from its worst features. The European Minister, Tristan Garel-Jones, was Welsh with an English seat and a Spanish wife and practically personified the Maastricht Treaty. He spent hours at the dispatch box arguing that the fears of the sceptics were exaggerated or unreal, but it was difficult to explain why we were expending this huge diplomatic and political effort on a treaty with so few positive virtues. The rebels by contrast could play on the accumulated fears of ground given up and powers exported, even if much of it derived from previous treaties. It was eighteen years since the 1975 referendum had endorsed British membership of what was then called the Common Market. Maastricht was now explicitly setting up a European Union with a political vocation, with various appendages such as the concept of EU citizenship.

The Prime Minister took the press criticism very personally and he clearly read all the papers every day. The previous summer I had been driving down from Scotland when I got a call on my mobile phone, 'The Prime Minister wants to speak to you'. I swerved on to the hard shoulder to receive an exasperated complaint about a defiant quote in a newspaper from Christopher Gill, one of the newer eurosceptics. There was little I could do, as the disciplinary powers of the whips office were largely illusory, but I promised the Prime Minister that a terrible fate awaited the miscreant MP. Gill became one of the rebel whips and later joined UKIP.

The committee stage ground on from January until April 1993, and eventually passed its Third Reading. But Labour had tabled a cunning amendment which would ensure that the Treaty could not come into effect without the Social Chapter, and this vote took place in July, right at the end of the parliamentary process. This was the key vote that would decide the matter, and the fate of the

41

government too. The Liberal Democrats joined with Labour, even though it threatened a European treaty they supported. Conservative rebels joined with Labour, despite their dislike of the Social Chapter. Only the Ulster Unionists were on our side. There were frantic preparations and calculations, and the arithmetic did not look good. Sick MPs came in by ambulance to be 'nodded through' in the courtyard without having to leave their stretchers. There were rumours of absent MPs being hidden in nearby flats to confound the predictions. At ten o'clock there were two divisions: the first vote was tied; the second, the crucial one, was lost by 8. Pandemonium broke out. The Prime Minister immediately rose to announce that on the following day there would be a debate on a Motion of Confidence in the Government, which, if won, would have the effect of ratifying the treaty. At this point the rebels backed away. Faced with the certainty of a general election if the motion was lost, they supported the government and it was carried. Thus ended one of the most bruising and debilitating episodes in British parliamentary history.

The third blow to the government in this torrid first year came from the coal industry. My old department had been abolished and the coal section had been absorbed into the Department of Trade and Industry, which completely misjudged the pit closure programme. Michael Heseltine was Secretary of State although he preferred the title President of the Board of Trade, which was strange as trade policy was by then largely determined by the European Union and there was no Board of Trade. Instead of continuing the incremental closure of uneconomic pits and voluntary redundancies, Michael announced, in concert with British Coal, the closure of 31 pits and the loss of 30,000 jobs, which was over half the remaining workforce. This included many mines in Nottinghamshire that had defied Arthur Scargill and continued working during the 1984 miners strike. It was also against a background of high and rising unemployment.

There was an immediate eruption of anger, not so much from the miners themselves as from the public, who felt that an heroic industry was being sacrificed by an uncaring government. There were marches, demos, critical sermons and hostile leading articles. Conservative backbenchers from mining counties made clear to the whips office that they could not support the policy. The Prime Minister decided on a brisk U-turn and, as I knew something of the industry, I got involved in brokering the necessary compromises to satisfy the MPs without spending too much public money. A review of the pits was announced, with extra money for the industry to help find markets for the coal and assist the areas affected by closures. The crisis passed but the government's popularity took another lurch downwards.

The government's political problems mounted but the economy was brightening, and by the spring of 1993 the recession was over. Norman Lamont was beginning to build a low inflation economy on the ruins of Black Wednesday, but on 27 May the Prime Minister sacked him as Chancellor of the Exchequer and appointed Ken Clarke. It was becoming a pattern of my life that when Prime Ministers or Chancellors went, something happened to me too. Sure enough, I was offered the job in the Foreign Office, whether as reward or revenge, as Minister for Europe.

Chapter 5

Minister for Europe

When you joined the Foreign and Commonwealth Office, you did at least get a good office. The original plan for a Byzantine building was rejected by Lord Palmerston as 'a regular mongrel affair', and was altered to the present classical style, which lifted my spirits every time I entered. My rooms overlooked the interior of the old India Office, the magnificent Durbar Court. Portraits of dead statesmen hung on the walls, some of which I changed, but I kept a fine marble bust of Lord John Russell, architect of the 1832 Great Reform Bill, which appealed to my Whiggish tendencies.

My duties covered Western Europe, Latin America and Security Policy. The Iron Curtain had come down four years earlier, but in the FCO it lived on as a division of responsibilities between ministers: another minister of state, Douglas Hogg, dealt with Eastern Europe, which included the Balkans, and I covered the West, which essentially meant the European Union. Douglas Hurd was immensely assured as Secretary of State, in a department he had joined as a professional diplomat 40 years earlier. The central role of the EU in policy making was now never seriously questioned. It was as much a part of the FCO universe as the continents themselves. The rough and unpredictable contingencies of public opinion, particularly as expressed in referendums, were avoided if possible. It was only later, under Labour, that the phrase 'British national interest' was dropped completely from the lexicon, but there was already a reluctance to assess policy options in that way.

Almost the first submission I read informed me of an EU fishing agreement with several countries in South America, including Argentina. The chief beneficiary was the Spanish fishing fleet with more money from the EU budget, and I questioned whether the interests of the Falkland Islands had been taken into account, as the fishing grounds nearby were in dispute. The answer was that the agreement had been negotiated by an EU committee, with participation by British officials, but the idea of using it as a lever against the Argentine claim had never even been considered. It was too late to change the policy, but from then on I was determined to keep a close eye on what was being done in our name, with our money, by the EU.

Although not particularly collegiate, at least with ministers, Douglas Hurd was very good to work for. The meticulous circulation of memos and files, which were all paper based then, ensured that everyone was copied in on everything, so we knew what was going on, and were given considerable latitude in carrying out our duties. The wounds of the Maastricht Treaty were still open in the Conservative Party and I saw it as my job to ensure that the safeguards we had negotiated were respected in practice. There were normally two European Council meetings, or 'summits', each year, although this later rose to four a year as EU government expanded. These were attended by the Prime Minister, Foreign Secretary, Europe Minister and sometimes the Chancellor of the Exchequer, and we normally flew from Northolt in an RAF plane. John Major never looked happy either before or during these diplomatic festivals, at which he usually had to fend off unwelcome proposals or generally spoil the party in some way. The first I attended, in Copenhagen, was better than most because it was mainly about enlarging the EU. This was a policy we supported, less for noble reasons of European unity, and more because we hoped that a wider EU would be less deep, and might also weaken the Franco-German axis.

For the next six months I was immersed in the negotiations to admit Austria, Sweden, Finland and Norway, travelling to each of them, receiving them back, and becoming a temporary expert on the law and language of EU treaties, which was a skill not to be

deployed at dinner parties. Each country was likely to be a contributor to the EU budget, so I hoped to recruit them as financial
disciplinarians. Sweden became a good ally against the euro, even
if this was thanks to the people (who rejected it in a referendum)
rather than the politicians (who mostly wanted it). Crown Princess
Victoria of Sweden was unmarried and in an idle moment I speculated about the possibility of a match between her and Prince
Edward, then unmarried, in order to cement a Baltic alliance – it
would have been a good idea in some earlier age when royal
marriages were seen as a branch of foreign policy.

In Finland I flew to Ivalo, well inside the Arctic Circle, to see the
vast tracts of virtually uninhabited country. The government was
keen to keep the area settled if only so that someone would notice if
the country was invaded. With Finland joining, the EU would be
acquiring an external border with Russia, and I spent a day with the
frontier police to see how they patrolled this 800-mile strip, which
proved much more secure than the borders of Southern Europe. Our
modernist embassy building in Helsinki was still bristling with
aerials and listening devices from the Cold War, only some of which
had been dismantled.

Norway was always a more doubtful candidate. Having broken
away from Sweden in 1905 its instinct for self-government was
strong, reinforced by its having been occupied during the war, when
its neutral neighbour was selling iron ore to Germany. Norway also
had oil and abundant fish, which were coveted by other EU
countries. Spain was, as always, determined and effective in promoting its own fishing interests, in contrast to the generally feeble
performance of the British Ministry of Agriculture, and this led to
prolonged negotiations about access to cod and herring stocks. Then
there was Norway's attachment to certain forms of whaling, which
was distinctly un-communautaire. I wanted Norway to join as she
would be an ally against bureaucratic uniformity and also, as a
longstanding member of NATO, would resist moves to make the EU
into an alternative military pact. But I was not surprised when the

47

people voted no to membership in a referendum; I would have done the same.

Austria, being a neutral country, was also suspicious of the EU's defence and security ambitions, and their foreign minister, Aloise Mock, who was battling against Parkinson's disease, became a good friend. It was always a highlight to visit Vienna, an imperial capital now servicing a small country of 8 million people, and they gave visiting junior ministers an extravagant welcome, with police outriders holding up the traffic at each intersection. The Austrian dossier was relatively easy to conclude and the country joined the EU in 1995, along with Sweden and Finland, but without Norway.

In between these talks I went to Brussels every two weeks for routine Foreign Affairs Councils. The FCO briefing was always immaculate and highly professional, and it was tempting to slip into a mode of working that saw the whole exercise as a search for bureaucratic consensus. The meetings started with a list of 'A Points' that had been agreed beforehand by the EU ambassadors and only needed to be rubber-stamped. Most of the rules and regulations that we agreed had the force of treaty law, so we were effectively legislating for an entire continent. John Major and Douglas Hurd had assured the House of Commons during the long Maastricht debates that the Treaty was a British success in establishing the primacy of member states, and that the drive towards ever more centralization had been halted. The law-making factory did temporarily slow down: Brussels was shocked by the first Danish referendum, which rejected the Treaty, and by the very narrow yes vote in France. But with the Treaty safely ratified, the tide came back in. Throughout this period, there was a persistent failure by British policy makers to understand the essential dynamic in Brussels towards greater centralization. Sometimes we won tactical victories, but this was rather like a fight on an escalator – you might win it, but you still arrived at the bottom. The European Parliament, whatever the views of the UK members, was always seeking more powers for itself and more money to spend. The book of EU directives and laws was getting fatter, but meanwhile the taxpayers of Europe were getting thinner.

Growth had stalled across the EU and unemployment was rising. The next two EU summits, at Brussels and Corfu, were dominated by concerns about Europe's faltering economic performance. Ken Clarke as Chancellor attended the Brussels summit and at one session he and I found ourselves representing the UK, instead of the Prime Minister and Foreign Secretary. The French in particular resented this, as they believed that politics should come before economics, and President Mitterand sent a note to the chairman that my presence was improper, but I remained at my post until the Prime Minister could be found. The outcome was in any case predictable: another action plan, a monitoring procedure, a proposed White Paper, a growth strategy, and more money for 'structural spending'. On the horizon was a proposal to increase the size of each country's contribution to the EU budget, which was to be the occasion for another bitter parliamentary battle at home.

I was anxious not to allow the EU to crowd out my duties in Latin America, and I did manage to visit that continent six times in my FCO year. My first trip was to Argentina, where the only real subject of diplomatic conversation was the Falkland Islands, which had been fought over 11 years before. For some reason I and my private secretary had to be booked under assumed names on the British Airways flight to Buenos Aires, so we chose Bentley and Craig, who featured in a notorious murder case in the 1950s. The meeting with President Menem went smoothly enough. We knew from various sources that his chief preoccupation at the time was how to change the constitution so that he could run for office for another term, rather than any new adventures against the Falklands.

The real business was done with Guido di Tella, the engaging Anglophile Foreign Minister who had a house in Oxford and well understood British attitudes towards the Falklands. He handed me in great secrecy a 'non paper' describing a scheme to pay each Falkland islander a very large sum of money, for which in return Argentina would gain sovereignty over the islands, which would however remain self-governing as regards their internal affairs. This presented me with a quandary because we had a strict rule not to discuss sovereignty with Argentina – to do so might draw us into negotiations, or unwelcome mediation efforts by outside bodies. However, I said I would take the paper back to London, where I discussed it with Douglas Hurd who agreed that such a cash offer could not be accepted even if, which we doubted, Argentina could raise the necessary money. As the scheme involved paying the islanders rather than the British government, it was decided that I should nevertheless consult them.

The following month, November 1993, I flew to Chile where I had friendly talks with the government, which harboured similar suspicions about Argentina. We then flew to Punta Arenas in the extreme south, where our assiduous Honorary Consul organized a party, attended by ruddy-faced descendants of British sheep farmers, members of the diaspora who had come to Patagonia a century before. A few hundred miles to the south lay the British Antarctic Territory, in a continent I had always wanted to see since reading the accounts of Scott and Shackleton and the heroic age of exploration before radios and mechanical transport. Our slice of territory radiated out from the South Pole and included the Antarctic Peninsula which curved up towards Chile and Argentina. All three countries had competing and overlapping claims so con-flict was always possible, particularly as Chile and Argentina had nearly come to blows over a number of other territorial disputes. None of this was quite urgent enough to justify an excursion this time, but ten years later I visited the Antarctic Peninsula on a private expedition with the family – an unbeatable experience.

Getting to the Falklands from Chile meant flying in a small plane round Cape Horn, as we were not allowed to cross Argentine air-space. Arriving at Port Stanley, the most obvious impression is also the most striking; its character is so British you can almost taste it. Despite our bashful reluctance about appearing patriotic, the brand is instantly recognizable when encountered 250 miles off the coast of South America. The following day was Remembrance Sunday and, as I drove to the service with the Governor in his London taxi, it seemed that the whole population had turned out to honour the dead. I was proud to lay a wreath in memory of those who had so recently died to defend the right of the islands to self-determination, in a war which had also ended the dictatorship in Argentina. I also visited a memorial to the first Battle of the Falklands, fought in December 1914, in which four German cruisers were sunk and I discovered that my mother's father had taken part as a midshipman on HMS *Inflexible*.

I stayed nearly a week in the Falklands, including a stay on a farm on the west coast belonging to an island councillor who had been forcibly taken to Comodoro Rivadavia on the mainland during the Argentine invasion. I also visited the memorial at Bluff Cove, the site of 48 British deaths when two landing craft were attacked by Argentinian Skyhawk fighters. We walked over the hills west of Port Stanley, similar in shape to the less rugged parts of the Scottish highlands except that they were covered not in heather but in a small shrub called Diddle Dee. The minefields near the coast were still fenced off, impossible to clear because of the peaty soil and the careless way they had been laid by the invaders. I did a broadcast and phone-in on Falkland Radio, pledging the British government's unflinching support, but saying we would help the Island Council in any sensible moves to establish more normal relations with its neighbour. To my relief, the councillors I consulted in private rejected the Argentine offer of cash for sovereignty and nothing more was heard of it. Guido di Tella reverted to a more conventional, and certainly cheaper, charm offensive and at Christmas he sent every islander a card and a video of Pingu the Penguin. I was content if Argentine efforts stabilized at this level, but until Argentina becomes a mature democracy the islands will always face a threat.

Over the coming months, I visited 12 other countries in Central and South America, to strengthen bilateral relationships which were often founded on strong historical links and a widespread appetite for learning English, as distinct from American English. I was shown the magnificent railway station in Sao Paulo which was designed and assembled in Glasgow, taken apart, transported to Brazil and reassembled in 1901 as the headquarters of the Sao Paulo Railway, which was itself British built and financed. There was also widespread appreciation of the role that Britain had played in the independence struggles of the nineteenth century. Unlike in Africa, where we were blamed for every conceivable colonial mishap, in South America we were on the side of the liberators, whose revolutionary heroes were often helped and trained by British governments. Cultivating these relationships seemed a better use of my time than spending hundreds of hours in Brussels arguing about strategic growth initiatives – particularly as many of these South American countries were growing faster than the rather sclerotic trade bloc that the EU had become. I also discovered that there were three African countries which each received more in foreign aid than the entire continent of Latin America, but I could not persuade Lynda Chalker, the aid minister, to alter this priority.

My other duties entailed visits to the external intelligence service, MI6, and to GCHQ, the intercept and listening agency, from where came daily reports to ministers about matters of interest. Sometimes we were the object of surveillance by others: an Argentine report of a private meeting I had had about the Falklands came back to me. More curiously, American Intelligence tracked a supposedly secret visit I made to Luxembourg. It was not often that I interviewed a prime minister about his suitability for a job, but in July 1994 I was sent to Luxembourg by our Prime Minister to see if Jacques Santer would be acceptable as President of the European Commission, taking over from Jacques Delors who was about to retire. The candidate backed by Germany and France was the portly federalist, Jean-Luc Dehaene, Prime Minister of Belgium, but John Major, with considerable courage and persistence, had vetoed him at the Corfu Summit. There was then a frantic search for someone else and the mantle of history fell on the unassuming shoulders of Jacques Santer (or Sancerre, as his critics called him, in supposed reference to his drinking habits). I interviewed him in his office, accompanied by

Michael Pakenham, our ambassador, who kept a checklist of pluses and minuses. Mr Santer evinced a sympathy for a federal Europe, but recovered by explaining that Luxembourg had been invaded and occupied in the Second World War, which also gave him an instinct for sovereignty. He thought that generally the EU should devolve more powers downwards, and that the Commission should, 'do less but do it better'. It was not an inspiring encounter but he scraped through and John Major supported his appointment. Four years later, Santer and the entire Commission resigned over mismanagement and corruption, but the fault was more institutional than any particular personal failings on the part of Mr Santer.

Another ad hoc mission was to Iceland, to represent the British government at celebrations to mark the 50th anniversary of the modern Republic. Iceland had broken away from Denmark in controversial circumstances in the Second World War, when Denmark was under German occupation. We gathered on the site where the Althing, the oldest parliament in the world, used to meet in a kind of open-air natural amphitheatre. As the sagas got under way it started to drizzle but our hosts had expected this and provided us all with umbrellas. Afterwards we repaired to a lunch hut, crowded with fellow European ministers and Scandinavian royalty. I briefly wondered about reviving my idea of an Anglo-Scandinavian royal match and thought of making some respectful enquiries about availability, but I quickly became confused about exactly which crown prince or princess belonged to which country, particularly as they all looked rather alike and were not wearing name badges. That evening there was a splendid dinner in Reykjavik at which I sat next to the leader of the Icelandic Women's Party, who was not amused by my flippancy. I have been back to Iceland several times since on various fishing expeditions, and I hope they maintain their sturdy independence and continue to patrol their own fishing grounds. They took a terrible hit during the 2007 credit collapse, but were able to recover because they still had control of their own currency.

Then there were the small residues of empire that gave disproportionate trouble. The dispute over Gibraltar simmered on. It had been a mistake to admit Spain to the EU without first insisting that she recognize the legal rights of the Gibraltarians to self-determination and the British Crown. Meanwhile a different problem had arisen: the British government had signed EU Directives on behalf of Gibraltar without having the power to implement them properly and this had now reached a crisis, with the EU threatening to fine the UK. Joe Bossano, the Chief Minister, was the most formidable negotiator I ever faced. He had a trained mind, a megabyte memory, and an absolute determination to put the interests of Gibraltar first. After lengthy negotiations, helped by intelligence gathering, we reached an agreement about financial oversight, but I could not help envying my colonial predecessors who could do this with less argument and fewer visits. Sometimes they hardly travelled at all: Sir Edward Grey was Foreign Secretary for 11 years until 1916 and only went abroad once; but he did fail to prevent the outbreak of a world war.

But however absorbed one might be in the partition of Cyprus or the defence of South Georgia, it was the division of Somerset or the shortage of local housing that bothered my local constituents. It is a good discipline on a minister in any government simultaneously to have a constituency and carry out the full duties of a parliamentary representative, and to find time on Saturdays for the advice surgery as well as the red boxes. For 23 years Caroline Usher, my parliament secretary, was the indispensable pillar holding up that side of my political life. The burden also fell on Linda and the family, but we did at least make good use of the holidays. In the summer of my Foreign Office year we took Jack, 13, and Matthew, 11, on a canoeing holiday down the Columbia River in Idaho, and the following year I combined an official visit to Ecuador with a family holiday on a boat in the Galapagos Islands. In view of what happened to Matthew later, I particularly treasure the memory of these days out of doors when we were all together.

At home, the problems of the government mounted, with the impression that we were gripped by a sleaze epidemic, although most of the allegations were disproved. John Major launched a 'back to basics' campaign but this unfortunately contrasted with the irregular private lives of some of his ministers, such as David Mellor whose affair with an actress was serialized in the *Sun*. And then there was Europe, which was sometimes dormant but never absent. When the negotiations on EU enlargement were nearly over, an incident blew up which nearly caused Douglas Hurd to resign.

Most decisions in the EU are taken by majority voting, and each country is allocated a number of votes – with more for the larger countries. This weighted voting system had to be adjusted when Sweden, Finland and Austria joined. They were each given a number of votes based on their populations, and this went through without difficulty. The problem arose over the definition of a majority vote. How many votes were necessary for a decision to be passed or blocked? Before enlargement, the blocking minority was 23 and the European Commission proposed raising it to 27, which would make it easier to get decisions through. This was resisted by the big countries, which wanted to stick at 23. Since the smaller countries had more votes than was strictly justified on population grounds, there was a fear that they could group together to take advantage of the larger countries. Thus the desire of Britain, Germany, France, Italy and Spain to keep the blocking minority at 23. But it was a fragile coalition. The Italians left at the first sign of trouble. The French appeared resolute and I was present when Foreign Minister Alain Juppé, on a visit to London, assured Douglas Hurd that they supported 23. But at some point the French and the Germans abandoned their position, without warning us. That left the Spanish, who were determined and tough. Our officials were not unduly worried, and thought that we would achieve an acceptable outcome by leaving it to the end. After all, each country had to agree to the Accession Treaty, so in theory we had a veto. This proved to be a seriously bad tactic.

Meanwhile, the stakes were being raised at home. Cabinet ministers from every department had been on the receiving end of objectionable EU legislation and did not want to weaken the blocking mechanism. So when things were slipping away from us abroad they were hardening at home. I went to an emergency meeting in the ministerial conference room in the House of Commons and gave a gloomy assessment. John Kerr, our ambassador to the EU and usually an astute tactician, made a misjudgement and talked up our chances. The ministers who were most insistent on sticking to the British position were Michael Heseltine and Ken Clarke. Douglas Hurd was told not to budge, and when the next Foreign Affairs Council meeting was deadlocked, a special meeting of foreign ministers took place in northern Greece to resolve the matter. All member states except Spain closed ranks against us. We were now holding up the accession of three countries whose membership we supported, over a matter that seemed only technical.

A messy compromise was eventually produced, which essentially raised the blocking minority to 27 but allowed that in certain circumstances there would be a delay for further discussions. At this point the Spanish, under intense pressure, gave way and accepted the new formula. Douglas Hurd only undertook to refer it back to the government. By now the press was in full cry and the Prime Minister had stoked up expectations by attacking John Smith, the Leader of the Opposition, at Prime Minister's Questions: 'We will not be moved by phoney threats to delay enlargement ... We shall not do what the Labour Party do, which is to say yes to everything that comes out of Europe ... The opposition would sign away our votes, our competitiveness and our money. The Rt Honourable Member for Monklands East (Mr Smith) is the man who likes to say yes in Europe – Monsieur Oui, the poodle of Brussels.'

A yawning chasm now opened up between rhetoric and reality. With huge reluctance, John Major accepted the compromise, knowing that Douglas would probably resign if the cabinet rejected it, and this set off an avalanche of hostile criticism about weakness, vacillation, and the impotence of British EU policy. It was a bizarre episode: the most pro-EU cabinet ministers had taken up the most inflexible positions on an issue of little practical importance. It turned out that few votes were actually decided by the majorities under dispute and the eventual compromise formula was hardly ever used. The same cabinet ministers had supported the Maastricht Treaty which transferred powers to Brussels on an industrial scale. There was clearly something wrong about our relationship with the EU.

I had been in the FCO for just over a year when the familiar government reshuffle got under way, with ministers nervously waiting by their telephones or waiting to see the Prime Minister. I was offered a job in the Treasury. One reason, explained by the Prime Minister, was that the legislation to increase the size of the EU budget was imminent and this would be a Treasury responsibility. It was thought (wrongly as it turned out) that I had enough influence with the expected Conservative rebels to ensure its passage through the House of Commons without calamity. I accepted the new job as the Treasury is the other great department of state and in many ways the centre of government. On 20 July 1994, I said goodbye to my private office, who had shown such loyalty and endurance and with whom I had flown several times round the earth, and crossed the narrow lane that separates the FCO and Treasury buildings on Whitehall.

Chapter 6

The Treasury

Leaving the gilded halls of the Foreign and Commonwealth Office, I entered what seemed like an asylum on the point of closure. The huge Treasury building on the corner of Parliament Street and Whitehall had some architectural merit viewed from the outside, but internally it was a mess, with bleak linoleum-floored corridors leading to high-ceilinged rooms full of old-fashioned desks and damaged furniture. I was amazed that the nerve centre of the British economy could look so scruffy, but assumed it was to set an example of gritty austerity.

In every other respect the Treasury was an elite organization, and its duties spanned not just taxation and spending, but the whole of economic policy. In some countries, like Germany, these responsibilities were divided between a finance ministry and a separate economics department. Tony Blair, in one of his doomed attempts to control Gordon Brown, hatched a similar plan in 2003 to split up the Treasury, prepared in secrecy under the code name 'Teddy Bear'. When Gordon Brown found out he objected, and that was the end of Operation Teddy Bear.

Ken Clarke presided over the department with genial gusto, and welcomed me, commenting that they could do with an accountant in the team. The sums were certainly large: the government was borrowing another £35 billion in the year I joined, which was modest by later standards but worried me at the time. I was Paymaster General, a title derived from the merger in 1836 of the offices of Paymaster of the Forces and Treasurer of the Navy. These had been highly lucrative positions as the holders were effectively private bankers for the biggest items of government expenditure, but the only vestige of this was that my signature appeared on several million cheques issued each month by the Paymaster's Office in Crawley. Then there were various ceremonial duties, quaint residues of our antique constitution. As a Commissioner of the Royal Hospital in Chelsea I went to Founders Day, where I met Sergeant Butterworth, who had been in my father's armoured car in the war and was now a Chelsea Pensioner.

My central responsibility was indirect taxation, mainly VAT and duties on alcohol, tobacco and petrol. I wanted taxes to be low, broad and simple, but this hardly described the British tax system, then or now. There was little chance of cutting the taxes I dealt with, as the priority was to lower income tax and we were still fighting the budget deficit left over from the recession. VAT had become a complicated tax, and thousands of ingenious and well paid tax consultants were constantly trying to find ways of avoiding it, particularly in the property sector. When the sums got too large, or when Parliament's intentions were clearly being frustrated, I could use a finance bill to block up the loophole. This of course made the system even more complicated, leading to more avoidance schemes, and yet more legislation.

Most MPs were not interested in the details of this fiscal arms race, but there were occasional rows over constituency matters. For instance, public transport was not subject to VAT, and it was found that a number of amusement parks were avoiding the tax by classifying their hot air balloons or steam train rides as public transport. They therefore claimed that they need not charge VAT on the price of the entrance ticket. I brought forward an Order in the House of Commons to stop this, and should have seen what was coming. It seemed that every MP represented an historic railway, a struggling train museum, or a charity providing balloon rides for disadvantaged children. I was even accused of wanting to put VAT on donkey rides on Cleethorpes beach (which they should have been paying already). I could only console myself with Edmund Burke's observation that, 'to tax and to please, no more than to love and be wise, is not given to men'.

Drink, tobacco and petrol were the familiar targets at budget time, and we were adept at finding non-revenue arguments for taxing them: health reasons for alcohol and tobacco; environmental reasons for fuel. These may have been the good reasons; the real reasons were revenue. Unfortunately, alcohol and tobacco duties were already much higher than in neighbouring European countries and this led to a big smuggling problem. Even without smuggling, people could quite legally cross to the Continent on 'booze cruises' and bring back as much as they liked for their own consumption. This cost us a lot of revenue but it did show the power of tax competition. If all such taxes were harmonized in Europe, it would stop the cross-border shopping but it would also remove the only really effective constraint on avaricious governments, which is that if they overtax, people can go elsewhere. So although I resented the loss of revenue, I did nothing to encourage EU tax harmonization.

A row over the EU budget was now to cripple the government. Member states paid money to the EU, supposedly in proportion to their relative prosperity. They then received money back for agricultural subsidies and to pay for EU industrial, social and employment programmes and so forth. Britain was historically a large net contributor, partly because of our small farming sector. Mrs Thatcher, by force of will, had achieved a British rebate which greatly reduced this imbalance, but by 1994 our net contribution had risen again to nearly £3 billion a year, at a time when public expenditure generally was being cut back. There was a legal limit on the size of the gross contribution from member states: it could not exceed 1.2 per cent of Gross National Product, but this deal had run out and the European Commission, the European Parliament and everybody else in Brussels wanted more. John Major, at the Edinburgh Summit two years before, had got an agreement to raise the limit in stages to 1.27 per cent. This was less than demanded by others and looked like a reasonable deal at the time, rather like the Maastricht Treaty, but on reflection it raised a number of questions. Why, if Maastricht really had checked the powers of the EU, did it need a larger budget at all? After all, the present formula allowed it to expand in line with growth and inflation. If national governments had to live within their means, why not the EU? The proposed new limit would cost Britain an extra £250 million a year at a time when the Chancellor was having to raise taxes at home. And then there was the problem of fraud.

Few subjects gave me more grief in those Treasury years than the administration of the EU budget. There was little accountability for it, no will to reform it, and only a grudging admission that anything was wrong. Some of it was outright fraud and the examples were multiplying of corrupt officials, diverted subsidies and phantom olive groves. It was difficult to know how much money was being stolen, because the accounting and record keeping was so poor. One year the auditors reported that they could not verify whether sheep premium payments in Greece had been properly paid because of 'bandit activity' in the region they wanted to visit. I sent a memo suggesting reform: instead of taxpayers in Britain paying money to the government, which then paid it to the EU, which paid it to the Greek government, which paid it to the sheep farmers, who then paid it to the bandits, why not do a deal directly with the bandits and cut out all the middle men? Not intended to be taken seriously; but then no one took the problem of fraud seriously either.

It was on my watch that the European Court of Auditors first refused to sign off the EU's accounts as being regular and legal. They have done the same in each and every year since, a terrible indictment of a rotten system. If the EU were a public company, all the directors would have been removed from office long ago and the firm wound up. A few years later, the European Commission under Jacques Santer did resign en bloc over accusations of corruption, nepotism and mismanagement. Then the EU's Chief Accountant, Marta Andreasen, blew the whistle on the chaotic state of the financial controls. She revealed that the EU accounts did not even use double entry bookkeeping, which was surprising as it was invented in Venice in the fifteenth century and became standard practice everywhere else in the world. Mrs Andreasen was sacked by Neil Kinnock, who was 'Commissioner for institutional reform';

a good example of shooting the messenger instead of heeding the message. Kinnock's own sad journey from critic to apologist showed how the EU was almost unreformable from within. The scandals continued, and some of the most spectacular frauds were later found at Eurostat, the EU agency with the responsibility for keeping the figures.

I raised the need for thoroughgoing reform in a series of Budget Councils, but only the European Commission could initiate legislation and nothing was done. Few other budget ministers took the matter seriously; most were content to issue ritual promises that all would be well next year. Sometimes the point was made that although the Commission was responsible for the £60 billion budget, most of the money was actually spent in member states and was therefore difficult to control. There was a simple answer to that: if there were concerns about any programme, it should simply have been shut down and the cheques stopped, but this never happened. We were always clearing up the mess instead of turning off the tap.

There was also a new 'Cohesion Fund' specifically for Spain, Portugal, Greece, and Ireland, to be divided up according to a predetermined formula. These handouts had a distorting effect on decision making in the EU, since the recipients would seldom challenge the main paymaster, Germany. The unearned cash injections were also creating a dependency culture in these countries, doing nothing to boost their long-term growth rates or productivity. Instead of being an incentive for reform, the subsidies became a cushion for inactivity.

This was the unpromising background to the legislation to increase the size of the EU budget. It also raised questions about the role of Parliament, and this constitutional point was energetically pursued by Peter Shore from the Labour benches, and Richard Shepherd from our own, and Tony Benn in his rational moments. Historically, the House of Commons had acquired the rights of taxation and the control of expenditure after struggle and civil war, but under the proposed EC Finance Bill, the House would be handing over a guaranteed stream of revenue for seven years. The money would be raised here and spent by the EU with no annual vote by Parliament or opportunity to recall the money or change it in any way. The Public Accounts Committee, which monitored government expenditure, would have no jurisdiction over how it was spent. This was not new, but it was getting more difficult to justify, and the disillusionment spread as the sums got larger.

The public was not very interested in foreign treaties, nor were most MPs, and nor were many cabinet ministers: Ken Clarke famously said he had not read the Maastricht Treaty. But people could understand money, and were asking why the UK was being told to pay over a large and increasing sum, more than any other country except Germany, when much of it was wasted, or at least not spent on things that we would choose. Public opinion, judging by the polls, was moving sharply against this, and so was the press. In ordinary times the Conservative Party would have benefited from this and would have stood for financial rigour and the rights of Parliament. But we were trapped in a system that was immune to change. There was no financial discipline and very little we could do about it. EU ministers did the deals which then had to be rubber-stamped by national parliaments.

Our parliamentary majority was now in single figures, worn down by defections and by-election losses. Amidst signs of rebellion, the Prime Minister and the whips decided to make the European Finance Bill an issue of confidence. That was the nuclear option, and if the government lost it would resign and there would be a general election. Government by suicide note is not normally a good idea but John Major felt increasingly hemmed in, and was already contemplating his own resignation.

The debate was not a great parliamentary occasion. The Opposition's line was to oppose the bill (which they supported) until more was done to combat fraud, even though their MEPs had all voted for a larger EU budget with no additional checks. Ken Clarke and Gordon Brown exchanged ritual insults and the only tension was about the size of the Conservative rebellion. I wound up the debate, making the point that Labour and the Liberal Democrats were opportunistically voting against a measure they really supported, but my heart was not in it. In the event the Ulster Unionists, whose dislike of the EU was only equalled by their dislike of Labour, voted with us and we won by 27. But 8 Conservative backbenchers had abstained and the next day the whip was withdrawn from them. This operation was not particularly painful for the miscreants, who achieved instant celebrity, but it created a headache for the government because its majority in the House now vanished altogether. A week later, there was a further rebellion and the vote to increase VAT on fuel was lost by 8 votes. The Liberal Democrats, who had advocated taxing fuel for environmental reasons, changed sides when public opposition mounted, confirming their reputation as the scavengers of politics.

As the government disintegrated, the economy improved. Released from the shackles of the Exchange Rate Mechanism, the Bank of England could set interest rates to suit the British economy. Growth picked up, exports surged, inflation was under control and unemployment fell. We became the best performing large economy in Europe, but there was no political dividend for the government.

Planning for the annual budgets included stays at one of the country houses given to the government by generous or childless aristocrats in the past. Normally we went to Dorneywood in Buckinghamshire, but once we stayed at Chevening in Kent, lent by Douglas Hurd as Foreign Secretary. The task was to fashion a budget out of the hundreds of 'budget starters', which were proposals for tax or spending changes on which the technical work had been done. For recreation, there was always a billiard table, and I introduced the Treasury team to an unconventional variant of the game called Freda, played by hand with special rules, at which the civil servants were soon winning.

These budgets, of 1994 and 1995, had to be cautious affairs as government borrowing was still high, but the economy was now growing strongly and this, to me, depended crucially on two things: avoiding burdens on business and setting our own interest rates. Neither of these conditions was secure.

The economy was living off the market reforms of the 1980s, which had been pushed through in the face of relentless opposition from the other parties, the trade unions and sometimes even business groups like the CBI. All the old state-owned industries were performing better in the private sector, and most other countries were following our lead. Michael Heseltine wanted to privatize the Royal Mail but a cautious John Major and a few timorous backbenchers scuttled it. The Dutch and German governments went ahead with their own sales, and secured better postal services as a result.

Meanwhile we were on the receiving end of a stream of EU regulations which the Maastricht Treaty had done nothing to slow down. Our opt-out from the Social Chapter was simply bypassed. For instance, the controversial Working Time Directive was re-branded as a Health and Safety measure and imposed on us by majority voting. So the hard-won freedom from excessive business costs and job-destroying regulations was being steadily undermined.

The other essential freedom, to set interest rates, was in evidence every month at the meetings between the Chancellor and the Governor of the Bank of England, Eddie George, attended by all ministers. The minutes of the meetings were published and became known as the 'Ken and Eddie show'. It was a normally harmonious act but when there were differences, Ken prevailed. A bolder government would have taken the next step and made the Bank of England independent. The real threat was that the government would give up all monetary independence by joining the European single currency. And that was a real possibility. John Major in his memoirs recorded that, 'Ken believed that the single currency would come into being, and that Britain should be part of it'. Ken was Chancellor and therefore had a lock on this policy. The official government line was not to rule it in or rule it out, but to wait and see. Apart from the Chancellor, Michael Heseltine and John Gummer were known to be in favour of joining; Michael Howard, John Redwood, Michael Portillo and Peter Lilley were against. I could not believe that a Conservative government could even contemplate giving up control over the economy, and as the public had similar doubts it was puzzling why we continued to prevaricate.

It was hard to divine exactly where John Major stood. He seemed to regard the whole European issue as primarily one of party management. He later described his attitude towards the EU as, 'a friendly agnostic', but this was not a very convincing guide to action. The EU was not a destination; it was a process, and it carried agnostics along with it, particularly the friendly ones. Given the damage that a failed euro would have on the British economy, it was extremely unfortunate that the government's paralysis on the issue prevented us warning other countries of the reckless way that the project was being promoted.

In February 1995 Ken Clarke made a strongly pro-EU speech at a European Movement Gala Dinner, asserting that monetary union did not mean giving up political powers. We were in the middle of taking the Finance Bill through the House of Commons, a bill which was the result of a great deal of discussion between ministers. But our policy on monetary union was never collectively discussed or, as far as I could see, analysed by officials. The written briefing for use at Treasury Questions treated the issue of whether we should give up sterling as a purely technical matter, without any mention of powers transferred or lost. This was plainly misleading. Ken Clarke's speech, and others like it, caused a great deal of unhappiness in the wider party, and a number of cabinet ministers commented publicly on the risks and objections to joining the euro, including Jonathan Aitken, who was a welcome addition to the Treasury as Chief Secretary.

In June 1995, John Major decided to challenge his critics and put an end to speculation about a leadership challenge. He announced his resignation as leader of the Conservative party at a press conference in the garden of 10 Downing Street, inviting his critics to 'put up or shut up'. In the leadership election that followed, only John Redwood challenged John Major; as a member of the government I felt I could not vote against the Prime Minister without resigning, and now was not the moment. The result was an unconvincing win for the Prime Minister and revealed a sizeable backbench revolt: John Major 218; John Redwood 89; Abstentions 20. John Major looked very gloomy the next day and the whole episode did little to shore up his crumbling home base. There was no change of policy, only more appeals to party loyalty.

In the Treasury, we returned to the business of planning the next budget, collecting taxes and controlling expenditure. Jonathan Aitken had resigned to pursue a libel case against the *Guardian* about whether he or a Saudi businessman had paid his hotel bill in Paris. His place as Chief Secretary was taken by William Waldegrave, who was formidably equipped to negotiate the complexities of a spending round, and he asked if I would help with the background work and deal with some of the smaller government departments. In February 1996, I was sworn in as a member of the Privy Council in a ceremony at Buckingham Palace. An official explained the choreography, which involved a certain amount of walking backwards, but I still tripped over a footstool and nearly collided with the Bishop of London, who was also being made a Privy Councillor. Very few privileges went with the title, but the Oath was good on defending home rule:

> You will to your uttermost bear Faith and Allegiance unto the Queen's Majesty; and will assist and defend all Jurisdictions, Pre-eminencies, and Authorities, granted to Her Majesty against all Foreign Princes, Persons, Prelates, or Potentates ...

As part of an attempted relaunch of the government, Michael Heseltine was appointed Deputy Prime Minister and First Secretary of State, with a remit covering the whole of government policy. Michael believed in active government, and the fact that the EU was now the biggest government of all, and the most powerful, attracted him. He acknowledged that there were forces in the EU opposing us, but believed they could be overcome, and that we could fashion an organization to suit British purposes. Each setback or disaster was seen not as a warning but as an argument for more Europe and

closer engagement. When I talked to him about the escalating problem of fraud and losses in the EU budget, he immediately agreed,
and proposed a basement-clearing reform of the way it was run,
which of course came to nothing. On the single currency, he was an
early and convinced supporter, so now the two most senior positions under the Prime Minister were occupied by dedicated Euro-
centrics, which to me was dangerous and increased the risk of a
coalition policy developing.

In March 1996, Europe struck again. The Ministry of Agriculture had set up a committee to investigate a cattle disease called
Bovine Spongiform Encephalopathy (BSE) and it had detected a
possible link with a fatal human brain disease, Creutzfeldt-Jakob
Disease (CJD). The risk was judged very small but it had to be
announced to the House of Commons, which detonated a huge
health scare. The press speculated that millions of people had
already eaten infected beef and would die over the next ten years
from 'Mad Cow Disease'. In fact, measures had already been taken
to eliminate the source of BSE infection in cattle, but Harriet
Harman, Labour's health spokesman, was determined to dramatize
the risk and blame it all on the government. Beef sales plummeted,
and the only solution looked like a massive cull of nearly all cattle.

The EU Veterinary Committee immediately imposed a ban on the
export of British beef, not just to the EU but to anywhere in the
world. Yet beef off the bone was now judged to be entirely safe to eat
in Britain. So British farmers could not export safe beef to non-EU
countries, even if those countries wanted to buy it. This was trans-
parently a political move by EU countries to protect their own
export markets. Three and a half million cows were eventually
culled, at a cost to the taxpayer of over £4 billion. Douglas Hogg, the
Minister of Agriculture, took most of the flak and showed com-
mendable courage. At the Bath & West Show, next to my constituency, he went ahead with a meeting with angry farmers whose
herds were being slaughtered, while a menacing crowd bayed
outside.

Despite these measures, the EU refused to lift its ban, even on beef derivatives like gelatine, which there was no scientific reason to ban at all. The Prime Minister felt bruised and betrayed by EU leaders who constantly promised a more rational policy and then failed to deliver. So the government adopted a policy of non-cooperation and announced that the UK would exercise a permanent veto against EU measures which required unanimous consent. This policy was strongly supported by Michael Heseltine, and even the Labour party joined in after reading the public mood. A month later the non-cooperation policy was ended, after we received some vague assurances about a staged lifting of the beef ban, but it was not completely removed for another three years, and even then France would not comply.

I had already decided to go. The elastic connecting my loyalty to the government with my doubts about the EU had stretched to breaking point. Vacillation about the single currency was now a government principle. We were edging towards membership of the euro. Constitutional questions about powers and accountability were being ignored or denied, and as a minister I was having to say things that I didn't believe. At the end of a conference for Ministers of State at Chequers I asked Alex Allen, the Principal Private Secretary at No. 10, for an appointment to see the Prime Minister.

Chapter 7

Resignation

I saw the Prime Minister on 16 May 1996 in his office in the House of Commons and told him I would resign over an EU policy I no longer believed in. I thought the direction of government policy was against British interests and was a threat to parliamentary self-government. Specifically, joining the euro would be a disaster on a scale much bigger than the unfortunate experiment with the ERM, and on something this important the government should make up its mind and oppose. As there seemed no chance of changing government policy from within, I wanted to campaign from without.

John Major listened to this in his usual courteous way and then brought the discussion round to the problem of party management: 'I see myself with one foot planted on either side of the fault line that runs through the party on Europe. I have to keep the party together or we risk disaster.' I countered that the great bulk of the Conservative Party, and a majority of the country, were against giving up the pound. We should make a virtue of having our own monetary policy, and a high growth rate to match – an election winning combination.

As I was adamant about resigning, John Major should have got rid of me that day. That would have shown who was in charge and put me on the defensive. Instead, he asked me to stay on until the next ministerial reshuffle in July, doubtless hoping it could then be presented as a minor change amongst many others. I agreed to do this, but for the government it backfired completely, as events were to show.

I went straight from the Prime Minister's office to tell Ken Clarke that I would be leaving the government in July, and would therefore still be one of his ministers for the next two months. Ken's views on the merits or perils of a single currency were strangely undefined. He seemed more concerned to stop what he regarded as a drift to euroscepticism than to engage in any debate about whether a single currency would work. He told me several times that a Conservative Party isolated from the EU would become very right wing and nationalistic. As well as brushing aside the economic objections, he simply ignored or dismissed without argument the political con-sequences of joining a single currency, and he would not admit that a currency union would require a political union as well, to control tax and expenditure. Whether this was from intellectual laziness or political prejudice, I could not tell. But he would not budge. The Chief Whip, Alistair Goodlad, was also told I had resigned, but only these three knew, and this secrecy was maintained until near the end.

The government's most pressing decision was whether Britain should join the euro, which was now certain to come into being. Under the terms of the British opt-out, a decision had to be made within a year. I was afraid that, as with the ERM, we would drift into a position of acceptance, with the only argument being about timing. The Labour party, now under Tony Blair, was increasingly keen on monetary union. The older eurosceptics like Peter Shore had been replaced by Peter Mandelson and a whole raft of New Labour designers whose support for the EU was a symbol of their break with old Labour. If they won the election I could see them taking us into the euro with the support of senior Conservative leaders and the Liberal Democrats, and winning a referendum on it too.

It is always vital to influence important decisions early, otherwise arguments are simply used to justify a course of action already embarked on. This is what happened with the Exchange Rate Mech-anism. The government's initial refusal to join gradually changed to a policy of only joining 'when the conditions are right'. This next became, 'yes, but not now'. Then we joined. Then it collapsed. But at least we could escape from the ERM. The single currency would be, in the words of the Treaty, 'irrevocable'. I therefore decided to write a pamphlet setting out the case against a single European currency. The arguments I used were not original, but culled from economic journals and from a look at history. The Treasury had a few papers on the subject of currency unions and the ever-helpful House of Commons Library found others. Working at weekends in my constituency, I pulled the arguments together and put them in a British context. If I could claim to have written anything of any perception and foresight, this was it.

A study of currency unions, in Germany, Italy and the USA, showed that they always *followed* the creation of a federal state. The United States had no unified currency throughout its early history and the Federal Reserve Bank was only founded in 1914, many years after the country was unified politically. Therefore the attempt by the EU to reverse this order and introduce a single currency *before* the creation of a federal union was without historical precedent.

Then there were the sobering lessons of more recent history. The 1970 Werner Report envisaged European monetary union within ten years, but the plan foundered when the Bretton Woods system, which had governed global exchange rates since the end of the Second World War, collapsed in 1971. The next plan was for a 'snake in the tunnel', whereby European currencies would move against each other within narrow limits, but this failed when the oil price shock of 1973–4 caused the economies of participating countries to diverge, and one by one they dropped out of the snake to float freely. This was followed by the Exchange Rate Mechanism debacle, already described. Each of these attempts at monetary union had been derailed by external events, commodity shocks, German reunification, or disturbances of one sort or another. These events were always unexpected, but always happened.

The obstinate and inconvenient fact was that the national economies of Europe were (and still are) varied and diverse. They had different growth rates, trade patterns, and economic structures. Some, like Germany, had highly productive industrial sectors. Others lagged behind, or depended much more on agriculture, or tourism, or subsidies. The UK had a dominant financial sector as well as being the EU's only oil exporter. These differences were deep rooted and persistent, and would not end just because the countries concerned joined a new currency.

A single currency squeezes all these different economies into the same mould. They must all submit to one interest rate and one exchange rate. If a country has a relatively high inflation rate, it cannot raise interest rates. A country wanting to lower its exchange rate, to boost exports or regain competitiveness, cannot do so. It is trapped. This could be disastrous in times of economic turmoil or when one of those regular but always unexpected shocks hit the eurozone. Without an adjustment mechanism, a country in trouble would face unemployment and falling wages, and might never regain competitiveness.

But what about the United States, a country with considerable regional variation, but with a successful single currency? Why would it not work in Europe too? The comparison actually destroys the case. America is one country, united by language, laws and historical experience for over two centuries. People move easily between states to live and find work. Many studies showed that labour mobility was lower within European countries, and lower still between them. Nor was labour mobility officially encouraged in the EU. The Commission described regional mobility of labour as, 'neither feasible, at least not across language barriers, nor perhaps desirable'. So that adjustment mechanism was absent in Europe.

America also had a large federal budget which acted as a stabilizer and helped to iron out the fluctuations between states. Would this be necessary in the EU? No one would say. The existing EU budget, at 1.2 per cent of GDP, was many times smaller than the American federal budget, and the agreement to increase it slightly had been very unpopular, not just in Britain. Germany knew that once the poorer countries could expect large cash transfers, they would relax their efforts to reform their economies or control their finances. A single currency would create a 'free rider' problem, with weak economies living off the high performers. Germany therefore

74

insisted on a 'no bail-out' clause, to prevent the EU becoming a transfer union, paying endless subsidies to the weak countries. So Europe did not have a large budget or transfer mechanism on anything like the scale of the American government. The American example showed that the conditions necessary for a single currency in Europe did not exist, and there were no plans to create those conditions.

By way of balance, the pamphlet also examined the economic case for a single European currency, which rested on the claims that it would lower transaction costs for traders and travellers, help complete the single market, and bring exchange rate stability. These benefits were small or illusory. Businesses could hedge against exchange risks, and the cost of electronic transfer of money across borders was cheap and getting more so. Nor had it ever been shown that free exchange rates were a barrier to trade. The huge increase in trade flows between Japan, the US and elsewhere had occurred despite regular fluctuations in the value of their currencies. As to exchange rate stability, it was of course possible to achieve this by abolishing the currencies altogether, but this would not remove the underlying strains, which, if suppressed, would burst out in a much more damaging crisis.

In short, the EU was not an Optimum Currency Area – defined as a geographical area where economic efficiency was best served by a single currency and where the attendant risks were manageable. The European Commission paper which advocated a single currency, called 'One Market, One Currency', dismissed such analysis. It did refer to the possibility of future divergence between the national economies but asserted that this could be dealt with mainly by, 'wage and price flexibility'. This would mean wage cuts for a country adversely affected by an external shock. But at the same time, the EU was passing ever more social and employment laws which reduced market flexibility. There was therefore a contradictory muddle between policies and aims.

The more I read, the more I understood that the single European currency was not really about economics at all. The real truth, sometimes admitted on the Continent but always denied at home, was that it was overwhelmingly a political project. Facts had to give way to the vision of a united Europe and economic logic was not relevant unless it served this purpose. And the fact that a single European currency would eventually need a single European state was thought by the zealots to be a virtue, though they were careful to camouflage this aim.

My pamphlet concluded:

> A single currency will have dire economic consequences which will create a new division in Europe ... A single monetary policy cannot deal with the differences, divergences and cyclical variations in the European economies. To have any chance of success it would require the completion of a federal European state with its own budgetary powers. This time, Parliament and the electorate must be aware of the real implications of joining a single European currency. We must say 'No' and say it now.

I sent the completed draft to the Centre for Policy Studies, whose energetic director, Tessa Keswick, liked it and started to prepare it for publication. Unfortunately the chairman of CPS, Lord Griffiths, reported the pamphlet to his fellow peer, Ian McColl, who was the Prime Minister's PPS in the Lords. McColl in turn told the Prime Minister and as a result CPS refused to touch it. I thought this was a spineless decision by a supposedly independent think tank and I told Lord Griffiths this in a heated telephone conversation, but he obviously valued his relationship with the PM more than any principle of free enquiry.

Time was now very short before the predicted reshuffle but the Bruges Group picked up the draft, and their printers did a heroic job in getting it ready on time. Meanwhile I had a last meeting with the Chief Whip, Alistair Goodlad, and Ken Clarke. They offered to extend my Treasury responsibilities to include monetary policy and planning for the single currency, and cannot have been surprised when I turned it down. I was told I would be known as a 'discredited traitor', but decided to take my chance.

On Friday, 19 July, there was a leak from the Treasury. Robert Peston of the *Financial Times* got the story, apparently from officials in the department, and I started to get calls in my constituency, but replied, 'no comment'. The Treasury press office was fielding enquiries and passing them on to No 10. The next day, the *FT* ran a fairly accurate story, mentioning a forthcoming pamphlet and the efforts made to stop me resigning. The *Daily Express* ran an 'exclusive' along the same lines, and the *Daily Telegraph* led with the story in late editions. At my morning advice surgery in Wells, journalists were spotted outside, or as my constituency agent put it, there were 'reptiles in sight'. Then the media circus moved to our village of Pilton, more usually known as the site of the Glastonbury pop festival, and staked out our home. It was a very hot day and Florence, 8, eventually took pity on them and gave them drinks. I rang Alex Allen, the Prime Minister's private secretary, and said I would be resigning on Monday, and escaped across a field at the back of the house to my next appointment.

On Sunday the newspaper coverage varied from the *Sunday Mirror*'s, 'Tories at war as Minister set to quit', to an overexcited *Sunday Express*, 'The man who turned the tide against Europe', plus some background pieces about the line-up in the cabinet: 3 in favour of the single currency (Clarke, Heseltine and Gummer) and 20 against – or at least willing to rule it out for the next Parliament.

The next day a TV crew hovered outside our house in London as my driver, Cyril Harbinson, picked me up for the last time. I told them I had a letter for the Prime Minister. At the Treasury I said goodbye to my private office who came down to the inner courtyard to see me off. As I drove to the House of Commons photographers ran alongside the car, banging on the roof and snapping through the window. My letter had now reached Downing Street and was on the one o'clock news, and Michael Heseltine was questioned about it in the House of Commons. A copy of the *Evening Standard* was lying in the library; its headline ran, 'Bombshell letter as minister walks out'.

THE RT. HON. DAVID HEATHCOAT-AMORY, M.P., *Wells*

HOUSE OF COMMONS
LONDON SW1A 0AA

Rt Hon John Major MP
10 Downing Street
London SW1

25 July 1996

Dear Prime Minister,

On 16 May I informed you that I wanted to leave the Government. We agreed that I should stay until the July reshuffle.

I am leaving because I can no longer support the Government's policy towards the European Union. At the Foreign Office and more recently at the Treasury I have dealt with the European Union at first hand. I have supported a policy of attempting to reform it and building a relationship which protects British interests and prevents unwarranted interference in our affairs. This policy is not working. The drive to political union in Europe is relentless and has already gone beyond what most people regard as acceptable.

In particular I am convinced that joining a single European currency would be disastrous, both politically and economically. I know we are not as yet committed to a single currency. However the Government's equivocation on this issue is confusing to the public and disappointing to most of our supporters. When something is clearly against the national interest, it is our job as the party of the national interest to make our position clear and resist it now.

I believe we must build a new relationship with the European Union. We can have free trade in Europe without being shackled to an economic system characterised by unnecessary regulations, high costs and unemployment. We can have close political relations with our European neighbours without submitting to a federalist legal system.

It is because I see a new relationship with the European Union as essential that I have resigned from the Government and intend to speak freely from the backbenches.

It has been a privilege to serve in your administrations. I will, of course, continue to give you my support and do my utmost to secure the Government's reelection.

Yours ever

David

The pamphlet – *A Single European Currency: why the United Kingdom must say 'no'* – was published the following day at a press conference in the House of Commons. It was sent to all MPs and newspapers and was reprinted two months later, its sales making the Bruges Group a good profit. As a concession to party manage-ment I did not make a Commons statement as resigning ministers normally did, and I only accepted some of the media bids that came in. On Channel 4 News I said that Ken Clarke had been a successful Chancellor, and a good judge of interest rates, which made it all the odder that he wanted to give it all away to the European Central Bank – a sad end to the 'Ken and Eddie Show'.

All the papers printed the resignation letter, and most comment pieces were favourable. Several suggested that the wrong Treasury minister had resigned. *The Times* saw the Prime Minister as para-lysed by a small group in the cabinet. The *Sun*, under the heading, 'Fight or you are a goner', challenged the Prime Minister to get off the fence, and went nicely over the top in calling me, 'The hero who put Britain first', though this was slightly spoiled by a snippet on another page headed, 'The toff who longs for the PM's job'. In the *Telegraph*, a letter from a reader in Tonbridge said, 'You published a photograph of Mr Heathcoat-Amory at his breakfast table. Can any person who permits a milk bottle on his table be considered for high office? In the circumstances his resignation seems appropriate.' Even my name came under scrutiny: Paula Yates – already mother to Fifi Trixibelle, Peaches and Pixie Geldof – had just given birth to her fourth daughter and was looking for names. The pocket cartoon in *The Times* had them consulting a dictionary, 'If you thought Heavenly Hiraari was bad, how about Heathcoat-Amory?'

There were kind quotes from friends on the back benches, and the Wells Conservative Association gave me a hundred per cent backing. The Chairman, Allen Cotton, wrote a letter saying, 'all true Britons should support him', which put a stop to any attempt to divide me from my constituency membership. Then the critics mobilized: the European Movement held a press conference at which Quentin Davies MP (later to defect to Labour) accused me of 'an extraordinary attempt to railroad No 10 into changing policy'. Edwina Currie declared that nothing must deflect the Prime Minister from joining the euro and said, 'the eurosceptics are in retreat'.

Charles Moore, editor of the *Daily Telegraph*, now published an article I had prepared about the wider objections to EU rule. I attacked the comforting illusion that the EU institutions would be satisfied with the powers they had acquired under Maastricht; they would be back for more. We were not 'winning the argument' in the EU: the cure for that idea was to spend some time there. The progressive transfer of powers was not only bad for democracy, it was bad government too and was undermining growth. 'How is the EU squaring up to the challenge of global free trade? Its response is to cling to an economic model which is visibly failing. The result is predictable: less employment. Europe is becoming a high-cost, high-tax, highly regulated continent. The people who are paying the price are the 18.5 million unemployed people in the EU.' It ended, 'The mutation of the European Union into an organization characterized by political interference and economic stagnation has created in Britain a crisis of public confidence. The causes must be understood and remedies found, or the disillusionment will be not just with Europe but with the democratic process itself. That is why I have left the Government.'

The pamphlet and the article received very fair coverage in newspapers and magazines and did at least generate some serious debate, though not in the cabinet. An NOP poll showed that only 20 per cent of people backed the government's wait-and-see strategy, and by two to one they said that if Mr Major ruled out scrapping the pound he would be more likely to get their vote. As the general election was looming ever nearer, this argument alone should have appealed to the Prime Minister. The *Sunday Times* observed that within months of the next election the government would have to make up its mind, so it was increasingly absurd to have no view before then. 'The government's position does not stand up to even a cursory examination.'

What was extraordinary was how the advocates of monetary union, or closer EU integration, avoided debate. They accepted that the decision on whether Britain should join the euro was the most important since we joined the EEC 25 years before, but they adopted a kind of herd mentality and simply ignored the political and technical objections which I and others wrote about. Our speeches, articles and pamphlets went unanswered. When challenged, they took refuge in generalizations about how Britain would 'lose influence' if we made up our minds about the euro. Or it was claimed that the situation was still 'evolving', when in fact the process was laid down in EU treaty law and the first two preparatory stages were already complete. I was also accused of being an extremist, a wrecker, and a Little Englander who hated foreigners. This was completely off target in view of my belief in Britain's global connections and responsibilities. It was the EU that I found narrow and introverted, obsessed by an outdated belief in regulation and central control. As to extremism, it was my critics who wanted to give up political and currency powers to the EU, thus reversing hundreds of years of British political development. I had the conservative aim of keeping the pound and retaining our powers of self-government, hardly an extreme position.

The philosophical roots of the EU could be found in the continental theory of the state as an idealized entity from which freedom and rights then flow. This might just appeal to a British socialist, but I was puzzled that those of a Conservative cast of thought could go along with it, abandoning a political tradition which starts with the individual and builds upwards to a limited state. People I otherwise admired showed the same collective myopia over the single European currency, apparently believing that it could be sustained without a massive transfer of powers to the centre. People who liked to call themselves moderates and pragmatists seemed in the grip of an ideology.

Parliament had now risen for the summer recess, but a mass of letters had come in. MPs know that letters are not necessarily an accurate measure of public opinion, but they are a good barometer

81

of how strongly people feel on particular issues. I received about 50 which were against and many hundreds in support, and eventually had to reply with a standard letter. I spent much of the recess writing articles for newspapers and assorted magazines, ranging from *Export Today* to *Chartered Banker*. In September, the opposition were sighted when fifteen industrialists signed a letter to the *Financial Times* saying that for Britain to resist joining a single currency, 'is based on a serious misunderstanding of the process of monetary union.' I wrote to each saying that on the contrary, the process had been analysed in detail and that the risks and costs greatly outweighed the possible benefits. I included a copy of my pamphlet and asked for their counter arguments. Five replied, referring me to the lead signatory, who didn't answer. Again, I was up against not so much an argument as an attitude.

I accepted speaking engagements from almost any group except UKIP, and some of them were quite well paid. The pensions industry chose the single currency as the theme for their annual conference and my co-speaker was Ted Heath, former prime minister and one of the architects of this new order in Europe, so I looked forward to hearing his case for the euro. On the platform he gave me a grunt of recognition and began his speech in 1957 with the founding of the EEC, post war reconciliation, British reluctance, and the need for bold statesmanship. He only got as far as about 1990 before concluding with the observation that the EU had always been primarily a political project, which didn't seem to advance the case for the single currency at all.

At the Conservative Party Conference in October, the Bruges Group organized a meeting, which overflowed. It attracted the interest of the foreign press representatives and a few days later the *Wall Street Journal* covered the subject prominently under the heading, 'Eurosceptics score a victory at Bournemouth'. The paper printed my speech, and its editorial judged that the Conservative party was overwhelmingly in favour of taking a stand against any further loss of powers or scrapping sterling. 'This was not a party deeply divided, but a few men [Major, Clarke] standing increasingly alone.' From a neutral source this was telling, and when I was back in London I visited the Foreign Press Association several times and contacted a number of publications in other EU countries to warn that the seductive embrace of a single European currency would end badly.

The main criticism that I and other critics incurred was one of disloyalty; that we were splitting the party and wrecking our chances at the next election. It is obviously true that a resignation is by definition a split but I did at least do it openly and gave my reasons. By contrast, most of the divisions on Europe that caught the attention of the press in the final year were within the cabinet. Unnamed aides or advisors, and mysterious 'friends of ministers', were briefing journalists about possible shifts in policy. There were reports of a plan to rule out joining the single currency for a limited period, which was then described as, 'preposterous' by Michael Heseltine. When the Prime Minister was challenged on this in the House by a gleeful Tony Blair, he backed the denial but always seemed to be searching for some new compromise on an issue which he agreed was of 'immense constitutional significance'. Then Malcolm Rifkind, the Foreign Secretary, declared on a visit to Bonn that he was, 'hostile to a single currency'. Ken Clarke responded that this couldn't be true, 'because he signed up to our policy'.

Maurice and Charles Saatchi, the party's advertising agents, came up with ideas to counter Tony Blair and the rebranded Labour Party, under the heading, 'New Labour: New Danger.' One of them showed Tony Blair in a black mask, and this 'Demon Eyes' poster achieved considerable notoriety. But it was nowhere explained exactly what these new dangers were. Mentioning an obvious one, quick entry to a single currency following a general election victory, was not allowed. The slogan, 'Euro Labour: Euro Danger', was vetoed. Our strategy was to try to demonize Tony Blair but not his intentions, and this didn't work.

Meanwhile detailed preparations for the launch of the single currency were going ahead in Europe. The Germans wanted strict limits on the borrowing and debt levels of the countries which joined, and these were set out in a Stability Pact. At French insistence, this name was changed to the Stability and Growth Pact, to make it sound better. It appeared that some of these rules might apply to the UK, even if we decided not to join, so it was a proper subject for debate in the House of Commons, but at this point the whips panicked and tried to stop it taking place, fearing a rebellion. The European Scrutiny Committee examined the proposals and said they should be debated on the floor of the House. A motion was signed by 150 backbenchers, demanding a debate. The government was now frightened of even discussing a subject on which it couldn't make up its own mind. Eventually there was a debate, which passed off without incident. The whole episode had created maximum ill will for no gain. The evasions and half truths continued.

The government was now in the evening of its life and postponed the election for as long as possible, hoping that the economic upturn would deliver it from annihilation. The election was eventually called for 1 May 1997 and allowed for a six-week campaign, the longest anyone could remember. All the polls were bad and I knew it would be a tough fight in Wells, as it always was with the Somerset seats. The anti-Conservative mood encouraged tactical voting to get rid of Tory MPs and this would help the Liberal Democrats who were never far behind. My chief asset was the Wells Conservative Association which, in every election I fought, gave me total backing from start to finish.

My Labour opponent was Michael Eavis, founder and organizer of the Glastonbury Festival which, despite its name, actually took place on his farm in Pilton. I had lived in the same village since 1985 and had been to every one of the festivals, which were getting bigger every year and usually overwhelmed the organization and swamped the facilities, particularly the drainage. Michael Eavis was a CND supporter, but we found other things to agree on at the candidate debates, and turned our fire on the Liberal Democrat from Sheffield, Peter Gold. There was also a Natural Law party candidate who had a bold policy of cutting £20 billion from the health budget

84

christening, with my
[fath]er and mother, and my
[old]er half-brother Michael
[and] sister Amanda, whose
[fath]er had been killed in
[the] war

On the boat coming home
from Egypt in 1951. As an
army family we were
always travelling

NATO flags: on a visit to Brussels in 1978 as a parliamentary candidate

Canvassing in Brent South (1979) with Joe Lynch of Coronation Street

ng ready for the 1983 campaign
ells, with the Young
ervatives

Flyposting in the 1983 election,
with Linda

Victory! Being carried out in traditional style at Wells

The things one does for the Party: a sponsored parachute jump over Devon

The family at home in the constituency: Jack, Linda and Matthew

Leon Brittan kept his appointment with the Wells constituency directly after the Brighton bomb attack in October 1984

AUTUMN 1984

WELLS CONSTITUENCY CONSERVATIVE ASSOCIATION

In Touch

Ted Heath coming to speak in Wells in 1985. For Ted, Europe was a vocation, not an argument

It wasn't all hard work: at a fashion show put on by friends in the Bishops Palace, Wells

eeting some of the Cheshire
omes residents, with my
ndon Marathon medal, 1987

With Cllr Neville Jones. As an
environment minister, I could
sometimes get extra help to
clean up dereliction in the
constituency (1989)

To David – with many thanks – Margaret Thatcher

Margaret Thatcher was always attentive to backbenchers and junior ministers – she sent me sever
letters of encouragement, and this photograph after she resigned

junior environment minister, 1989

DHA by Ian Nuttall, 1990
(© *Palace of Westminster Collection*)

M the Queen about to greet the King of Norway on a state visit to Edinburgh in 1994 (*DHA second
m right*). Norway voted no to joining the EU in the same year

With President Menem of Argentina in 1993. His offer of cash for sovereignty over the Falkland Islands was not acceptable

But I had to relay the offer to the Falklands. Here, the Military Commander and the Governor leav for the Remembrance Day service

As Paymaster General in 1995, signing one of those large cheques

hn Major answering
uestions in the House of
ommons. (*Left to right*)
chard Ryder, Tony Newton,
nathan Aitken, George
oung, Ken Clarke, DHA,
ony Nelson

Cartoon by Pugh in July 1996. Paula Yates – already mother to Fifi Trixibelle, Peaches and Pixie Geldof – had given birth to a fourth daughter and was thinking of names
(© J. Pugh, NI Syndication)

"IF YOU THOUGHT HEAVENLY HIRAANI WAS BAD, HOW ABOUT HEATHCOAT - AMORY ?"

Resignation, July 1996. The dangers of the euro were being ignored; it was the Cabinet that was unbalanced (© Garland, The Daily Telegraph)

01 family group; DHA with
k, Linda, Matthew, Florence
d our dog, Pippin

Matthew, in good times
(2001)

2001 election campaign, with Conservative branch chairman Bob Filmer. Note the Keep the Pound poster

Outside the European Parliament building, the monument to the euro, now tarnished

e Convention on the Future of Europe. Chairman Valéry Giscard d'Estaing, with Vice Chairmen
uliano Amato and Jean-Luc Dehaene. Alternative futures were not considered

oking for allies in the Convention: with the Estonian delegate (2002)

The *Sun* sent all its readers this pop version of my pamphlet about the European Constitution (2003)

Before my luck ran out: election victory 2005, with Linda

by hiring 7,000 experts to teach Transcendental Meditation and Yogic flying. Less welcome to me was a Referendum Party candidate, bankrolled by Sir James Goldsmith, who insisted on standing against me despite my known euro-critical views.

I knew the Labour Party was going to win nationally when two people on the doorstep, in separate Conservative voting areas, said spontaneously, 'I like Tony Blair'. After 18 years in office we, by contrast, looked ragged, tired and sleaze-ridden. It was also bad luck that the marital infidelities of three more Conservative MPs were reported in the opening weeks of the campaign. Europe did not feature particularly prominently as an issue until it was discovered that well over 100 Conservative candidates, including several ministers, had put in their election literature a promise that they would not sign up to a single currency in the next parliament. As this literature was printed centrally Michael Heseltine wanted to block it until the offending paragraphs were taken out, but this idea was wisely abandoned. Instead, John Major did an impassioned election broadcast appealing for indecision: 'Like me or loathe me, do not bind my hands when I am negotiating on behalf of the British nation'. It came over rather well, and certainly fresher and more spontaneous than the laboured compromises on which the policy rested. It was also disingenuous as all the preparation for the European single currency had been done. What was needed was a decision, but it was too late for that.

The election outcome had a ghastly inevitability about it, but even then the result was a shock: 178 Conservative MPs lost their seats and Labour won its largest ever parliamentary majority. Were the divisions in the party over Europe the main reason we lost? No, but the indecision and lack of clarity added to the perception that it was a party that had lost the will to govern. A Conservative policy of keeping the pound and asserting our financial self-government could have banished the ghost of Black Wednesday and reinforced the message that the British economy was now the best performing in the EU. It might not have saved us from defeat but it would have limited the carnage.

In Somerset we lost Taunton, and my neighbour Mark Robinson lost Somerton and Frome by 130 votes, a result definitely attributable to the Referendum Party and UKIP, which between them got nearly 3,000 votes. In Wells, the Referendum Party received just over 2,000 votes and I hung on with a majority of 528.

Parliament met the next week and when I stood in the crowded Members' Lobby I hardly recognized anyone. It was all going to be different, and, because John Major had resigned immediately, we had to elect a party leader and put together a new programme out of the rubble.

Chapter 8

Opposition

Opposition is hell, particularly if unrelieved by any serious prospect of winning the next election. All that lay ahead, but at least we started with a leadership election, and the chance of a fresh start. Two obvious standard bearers for the right and left of the party had already been eliminated: Michael Portillo had lost his seat and Michael Heseltine had just had a heart attack. Ken Clarke was first in the ring, followed by Michael Howard who had apparently secured William Hague as his running mate. Then Hague pulled out of the deal and announced he was running himself, which presented me with an acute dilemma. Michael was a friend and someone I admired as tough and decisive in office, but I was also sure we needed a clean break with the Major years and Hague, 36 years old, offered youth and an element of surprise. I declared for Hague and joined a boisterous launch party in Victoria Gardens next to the House of Commons.

It was the last leadership election to be decided entirely by MPs. Ken Clarke led in the first two ballots, just ahead of William Hague, with John Redwood in third place. John Redwood's campaign was hard hitting and personal. He sent a letter to us about Europe, saying, 'We shall <u>never</u> join a single currency', and enclosing quotes from William Hague where he had been less emphatic: 'William Hague, in his interviews, leaves open the possibility of a much more powerful European Parliament replacing our national democracy. On the Today programme he again refused to say Never to the abolition of the pound.'

Then, a week later, just before the third and final ballot, we all received an astonishing letter, jointly from Ken Clarke and John

Redwood, proposing a pact between them: 'If, contrary to our current expectations, progress was to be made towards a strong single currency and British entry became an active possibility, we would then undertake collective discussions in order to see whether we were agreed on where British interests lay. If we could not agree, we would have a free vote on the subject.' John Redwood urged his supporters to vote for Ken, and in return he would become Shadow Chancellor of the Exchequer. This extraordinary alliance was stillborn; most of John's supporters instead voted for William Hague who won convincingly in the final round.

William offered me the post of Shadow Chief Secretary to the Treasury. Peter Lilley, who had been a leadership contender, was Shadow Chancellor, and we set about learning the business of opposition. Peter was effective in the House, but no one pays much attention to Opposition spokesmen just after an election. We were also wrongfooted over Gordon Brown's early announcement to make the Bank of England independent. Although not a natural publicist or phrase maker, I could take some credit for establishing that the government had inherited a 'golden economic legacy'. Labour tried to claim that high growth and low unemployment all started on 1 May, in Year One, Era of Blair, but of course these achievements originated months and years before in our struggles with public expenditure, the privatizations, the control of regulations and taxes, and the taming of trade union power, all of which had been opposed by Labour.

In his first budget, Gordon Brown started to live off this legacy. After noting that, 'pension funds are in substantial surplus', he removed dividend tax credits from them, which cost them £5 billion a year. Over the next decade, as lives got longer and pensions got smaller, this pensions raid was exposed as reckless and short-sighted, but at the time no one listened. The CBI was notably supine in its dealings with the new government, and the Labour spin machine was already expert at swatting enemies and rewarding collaborators.

This attack on pension funds was not revealed in the Chancellor's budget speech; instead it was dressed up as a reform of corporation tax. It was ignored altogether in the pocket edition of the budget distributed free to the public. It was the first of the 'stealth taxes'. That phrase took off and is now in the Oxford English Dictionary, and there was some comment about its origin and first use. The truth is that when I joined the shadow cabinet, I thought I should find out what my opposite number, Alistair Darling, had been saying, so I went through the ordeal of actually reading some of his old speeches in Hansard. Buried in pages of deadening prose I spotted a quote in a debate on the 1997 Finance Bill, referring to National Insurance contributions as 'a back-door stealth tax'. I thought the term suited Labour very well. The Americans had invented a Stealth Bomber which could evade radar and this had been in the news. The phrase also rhymes with 'wealth tax'. So I adopted it and repeated it, and 'stealth taxes' eventually became part of the political language.

The government was next hit by a boomerang that they had thrown themselves. In the election they had campaigned vigorously against, 'Tory sleaze'. Tony Blair had taken a priestly stand and promised that he and his government would be 'purer than pure', and no suspicion of impropriety would be tolerated. That lasted just a few months. In October 1997, Bernie Ecclestone, boss of Formula One racing, asked for a meeting with Blair to lobby against the ban on tobacco advertising, promised in Labour's manifesto. Accompanied by Max Mosley, President of the International Racing Federation, he met Blair at Downing Street and the policy was immediately altered to exempt car racing from the advertising ban. The following month it was discovered that Bernie Ecclestone had given a million pounds to Labour before the election and had promised another million, not yet paid. A row erupted and eventually Blair went on TV to defend himself with the phrase, 'I am a pretty straight sort of guy'. Labour was told by the Committee on Standards in Public Life to pay back the donation, so lucky Bernie not only got the tobacco ban reversed but got his million pounds back as well, which helped explain why he was so successful.

A bigger skeleton rattling round in the Labour cupboard was Robert Maxwell, publishing tycoon and ex-Labour MP who had died in mysterious circumstances on his yacht five years before. After his death it was found that Maxwell had used hundreds of millions of pounds from his companies' pension funds to prop up the shares of the Mirror Group. Some of the print workers whose pensions he had stolen lived in my constituency and I got involved in the campaign, eventually successful, to make up the deficit from other sources. The question was, did the tentacles of the defunct Maxwell empire extend into New Labour? I got on to this trail, which ended in Peter Mandelson's resignation from the cabinet and an extraordinary cover-up by the Department of Trade and Industry.

Geoffrey Robinson had been MP for Coventry North West since 1976 but had spent most of his time building a career in the car industry, and had founded a company, TransTec, to exploit industrial inventions. Most of his private wealth came from an exotic Belgian woman, Madame Bourgeois, who had recently died, leaving Robinson £9 million. This money went into a family trust called Orion, based in Guernsey. Robinson was made Paymaster General in the new government and was a close confidant of Gordon Brown who was impressed by that rare organism, a Labour minister who could speak the language of business. It all went wrong very quickly.

Some of Geoffrey Robinson's shares in TransTec were held in the same offshore trust, Orion, and this was spotted by the press. Gordon Brown had said, just before the election, 'A Labour Chancellor will not permit tax relief to millionaires in offshore tax havens.' This now exactly described one of his own Treasury ministers. Hypocrisy aside, Robinson had not revealed that he had an offshore family trust to the Treasury Permanent Secretary, Terry Burns, as he should have done on becoming a minister. Robinson threatened libel action against the newspapers which reported this but that turned out to be bluster. Sympathetic journalists took the line put out by Alastair Campbell, the Prime Minister's press spokesman. Peter

Riddell wrote in the *Times*, 'Robinson's real crime is being a successful businessman and a multimillionaire who is a member of a Labour government'. In the *Independent*, Polly Toynbee complained he was being persecuted by Rupert Murdoch who was much worse, whereas Robinson was 'an honest man'.

Geoffrey Robinson received a mild rebuke from the House of Commons Standards Committee for not registering the Orion Trust in the Register of Members' Interests. But the episode had revealed an interesting connection with Robert Maxwell, because TransTec turned out to be a Maxwell company. Geoffrey Robinson had met the Labour tycoon in 1986 at a Labour party conference and Maxwell made Robinson a director of several of his engineering companies. Robinson had not declared these in the Register of Members' Interests. I decided to investigate all this, but at once ran up against a serpentine complexity of the Maxwell empire. Companies were merged, demerged, changed their names, issued subordinated loan rates and special shares, and had multiple overlapping directorships. Maxwell had given money to the Labour Party, and two Labour ministers, Helen Liddell and Lord Donoughue, had held senior positions in the Maxwell group.

To unravel exactly what had happened in a group that was now bust, I was greatly helped by David Shaw, who had been MP for Dover until the election and was also a chartered accountant. We found that Geoffrey Robinson had been chairman of a company called Hollis plc, of which the accounts said, 'The ultimate holding parent is Maxwell Foundation, a trust organised under the laws of Lichtenstein.' The 1999 published accounts showed that Robinson had been paid a £200,000 management fee which he had not declared. At my request, the Commons Committee on Standards launched another investigation, and Robinson simply denied that he had ever received or asked for the £200,000. The Committee, with its Labour majority, did not look for the documentary evidence that the money had been paid (though the proof existed, as will be shown). Instead the Committee concluded, 'We believe the relevant entry in the published accounts [of Hollis] is false', but they did observe that, 'the state of affairs revealed by the Commissioner's investigation reflects poorly on the chairman, directors and others responsible for producing and approving Hollis' accounts and their accuracy.' Although Robinson had escaped again, the press were not kind. Tony Blair cancelled his summer visit to the Robinsons' house in Tuscany, but Gordon Brown and his advisor Ed Balls remained doggedly loyal to the Paymaster General.

I wrote at once to the Registrar of Companies, pointing out that Geoffrey Robinson's defence was that Hollis' published accounts were false and therefore he, as chairman, had signed and filed false accounts, which was a criminal offence. The Registrar wrote back that, 'in the circumstances' it would not be appropriate for him to investigate and that he had passed my letter to the Department of Trade and Industry for reply. Two months later I got a letter from the new Secretary of State at the DTI, Peter Mandelson. 'The matter which you raised is being considered', and he launched an enquiry. This meant that one government minister was being investigated by another. When Peter Mandelson signed that letter he was unknowingly signing his first political death warrant.

Two years before, Peter Mandelson had been looking for somewhere better to live, and in his upwardly mobile way that meant Notting Hill. The house he found was much too expensive but Geoffrey Robinson lent him £373,000, unsecured and at a low rate of interest. There was nothing wrong with that. But when Mandelson became Secretary of State at the DTI he was obliged, under the Ministerial Code, to tell his Permanent Secretary about anything which might lead to a conflict of interest. Mandelson did not disclose the loan. And now he was investigating the business affairs of Geoffrey Robinson, a fellow minister from whom he had borrowed a large sum at a preferential rate. The conflict of interest was glaring. But the loan was a private matter between two MPs, and would have remained secret if Peter Mandelson had not been betrayed by his own party.

When New Labour was born, it had one enemy, the Conservative government, but by 1998 it had split into two armed camps, the

Blairites and the Brownites. The memoirs published much later, after Gordon Brown's defeat in 2010, showed in terrible detail their quarrels and rivalries. Brown's acolytes reserved a special hatred for Mandelson who had changed sides in the Labour leadership contest and got Blair in. Geoffrey Robinson was of course a Brown supporter and he told a number of tribal members about his loan to Mandelson, and this was leaked to Paul Routledge who was writing a book on Gordon Brown. The conduit was probably Charlie Whelan, the laddish and indiscreet spokesman for the Brownites, though this was never proved. Tony Blair wrote later, 'Whoever it was had done it with complete malice aforethought. This was not a story, it was a political assassination, done to destroy Peter; but it was also done to damage me and damage me badly, without any regard to the impact on government.'

The *Guardian* broke the story and then it was headlined everywhere. Blair prevaricated and tried to save his friend. His promise that the new government would be 'purer than pure' was forgotten. Mandelson toured the broadcasting studios, claiming that he had 'insulated' himself from the DTI enquiry, and that it was Robinson who had wanted to keep the loan secret. I toured the same studios, to keep the story focused on Mandelson's letter to me, the conflict of interest, the breach of the Ministerial Code, and Labour's double standards. The press kept up their assault, with the *Daily Mirror* particularly vicious. Six days after first considering the matter, the Prime Minister saw that the game was up and on 22 December 1998 told Mandelson he had to go. This was the first Peter Mandelson resignation. Two years later he resigned again from the government, that time over an allegation that he had procured a passport for a rich Indian businessman who had put money up for the Millennium Dome. After that he was appointed a European Commissioner, beyond the reach of the tiresome necessities of election or accountability.

To even things up, Geoffrey Robinson was sacked from the government as well. Although I had been instrumental in their forced resignations, neither Mandelson nor Robinson seemed to bear me a personal grudge and I had several amicable conversations with them afterwards. I was doing my job in opposition. Their real enemies sat behind them on the Labour benches. But there was unfinished business. What had happened to the DTI enquiry which I had demanded into the Robinson companies and the link with Robert Maxwell? After Peter Mandelson had confirmed that the matter was being considered, I had written him three more letters detailing the asset stripping, false accounting, and the money owed to pension funds and the Inland Revenue. I asked that this be investigated under Section 432 of the Companies Act, allowing for full disclosure. I was now to come up against the brutal methods of New Labour and how it operated.

By contrast with Margaret Thatcher, who carried out her revolution through the established civil service, New Labour was determined to capture the machine itself. They set out to dominate all the organs of government and were ruthless in their use of patronage and appointments. The law was changed to allow Alistair Campbell, the Prime Minister's spokesman, to give orders to civil servants. The number of special advisors, who were party appointees but paid by the state, more than doubled in a few years. These advisors moved into the press and publicity departments. Jo Moore, special advisor to Stephen Byers, famously tried to use the attack on the World Trade Centre as, 'a very good day to get out anything we want to bury'. New Labour's chief project was always its own survival.

This background helps explain the ensuing cover-up. Stephen Byers had taken over from Mandelson as Secretary of State at the DTI and a veil of secrecy fell over the investigation. He would not disclose who had set it up, when it would report, or whether it would be published. My request to Arthur Andersen, the administrators of the Maxwell companies, to examine the books and records myself was turned down. This was odd because an accountant called Michael Stoney (struck off as a chartered accountant for professional misconduct) had been allowed to do so on Robinson's behalf.

94

The DTI Inspector was actually Hugh Aldous FCA and in the course of his investigation he found what had previously been concealed: the evidence that Geoffrey Robinson had received £200,000 for services to Hollis plc. A year earlier, the House of Commons Standards Committee had concluded that the money had not been paid and the accounts of Hollis were wrong. In fact, Robinson had submitted an invoice for the amount on the letterhead of Orchards, his house near Godalming, Surrey. It had not been paid immediately because Robert Maxwell, battling for survival, was short of cash. But it was approved and on the invoice was written, 'paid'. The actual paying company was another in the Maxwell Group, Pergamon, which then recharged Hollis. The bank statements had been destroyed but the cash book entry showed the £200,000 paid to Robinson. The Committee on Standards had been misled, and Robinson's denials were false. But at this stage only the DTI knew this.

On 12 October 1999, I wrote again to Stephen Byers pointing out that it was 15 months since I had first raised the question of mismanagement and false accounting in the Maxwell-Robinson companies. Byers replied, 'My officials inform me that the enquiries you refer to are still continuing. The extent to which the papers may be disclosed depends on the nature of the case itself and other considerations such as the applicable law and commercial confidentiality. Subject to these constraints I would wish to be as open as possible on these matters. I hope this is helpful.' The sarcastic last sentence warned me of what was to follow.

On the last day before the Christmas recess, 21 December 1999, Byers answered a planted written question from a Labour backbencher, Ian Pearson, who had been Robinson's PPS: 'These enquiries have now been completed and the solicitors acting for my hon Friend the Member for Coventry North West [Mr Robinson] have been informed that the Department does not propose to take any further action.' That was all. They were burying the whole affair. I was not sent a copy of the parliamentary answer, or any letter of explanation. Three days later, TransTec, which was one of the companies I had complained about, was suspended on the stock exchange and was declared bankrupt, owing £129.5 million. A statement issued by the company said that two directors had resigned after failing to tell the board or the auditors about a large claim by an overseas customer.

The Department of Trade and Industry and its officials had succumbed to party political influence and had set up the enquiry in such a way as to prevent publication. It was certainly a cover-up. I had specifically requested an open enquiry. The department had suppressed information discovered by the Inspector, Hugh Aldous, which was of direct interest to a select committee of the House. There it would have rested if Tom Bower had not published a book the following year, *Paymaster*, which supplied the missing detail. Bower is a useful corrective in British public life: if someone's behaviour becomes too deplorable, he writes a book about them. In researching for *Paymaster*, he discovered the documents behind the undeclared £200,000 payment from Hollis, via Pergamon, to Geoffrey Robinson. With that information, the House of Commons Committee on Standards reopened its enquiry, and this time there was no escape. They found that Robinson had received the £200,000, had failed to register it, had failed to provide full answers during the 1998 investigation, and, 'Mr Robinson had additionally misled the Committee by denying that he had agreed or solicited the £200,000 fee.' The chairman of the Committee, George Young, observed that this was the fourth time that the Committee had upheld complaints against Geoffrey Robinson, and recommended he be suspended from the House for three weeks. Thus ended a disagreeable saga, but I had evened up the score against the government and put a splinter into the moralizing facade of New Labour.

The more routine business of opposition for me was to serve on each successive Finance Bill committee, where we won some tactical victories, and occasionally got some concessions, but the political dividends were very meagre. The usual problem of Labour governments – being good at spending money, but bad at making it – had been temporarily solved by selling licences for the next generation of mobile phones in 2000. This auction, the biggest ever held, netted the government £22 billion. Meanwhile, the golden economic legacy meant that Britain was growing faster than any other European economy, inflation was under control and unemployment low. Our warnings about squandering this legacy by overtaxing and over spending were ignored or ridiculed. The only serious wobble in the government's popularity followed a big increase in fuel duty which triggered a haulier's blockade of oil refineries, after which some opinion polls showed a Conservative lead, but a very temporary one.

The government made a more serious mistake, which lay like an unexploded mine, in failing to regulate financial services properly. I led the opposition on the Bank of England Bill and the Financial Services Bill which set up the structure of city regulation. We spotted the weakness in having three overlapping bodies responsible for financial markets: the Bank of England, the Financial Services Authority, and the Treasury. I was told by a minister not to worry because there would be a 'memorandum of understanding' between them to deal with any eventuality. Ten years later, when the Credit Crunch laid waste the banking system, this memorandum could evidently not be found. I cannot claim to have foreseen the 2008 crisis, but I regret not making more of the misgivings that I did have.

On Europe, there had been a kind of crossover between Tony Blair and Gordon Brown. Before the 1997 election, Blair had sensed the unpopularity of the euro; thus his article in the *Sun*, 'Why I love the pound'. Brown though was attracted to the single currency as an external discipline, fearing the spending demands of his own party. In office, this reversed. Brown saw the economic dangers and wanted to keep all the levers under his own control or that of the Bank of England. It was now Blair who wanted to join, and left to himself would have done so, egged on by Peter Mandelson, who advocated an early referendum on the principle of joining the euro while the government's stock was still high. To keep control of the policy, Brown invented five economic tests by which the government, in other words he himself, would judge whether Britain was ready to join. Charlie Whelan, Brown's personal press spokesman, started briefing newspapers that his boss was against joining, which was a breach of the parliamentary rule that important policy announcements should be made to the House of Commons, where the policy could be questioned. In October 1997, Brown was ordered to the House and declared, 'The decision on a single currency is probably the most important question that this country faces in our generation.' He reiterated his belief in a single currency – 'We are the first government to declare for the principle of monetary union' – but found that the British economy had not converged sufficiently with the rest of Europe to make it safe to join in the first wave. Instead, he committed us to a programme of preparation for later entry, complete with 'regional and sectoral conferences' for businesses. He concluded, 'It is therefore sensible for business and the country to plan on the basis that, in this Parliament, we do not propose to enter a single currency.' This was one of the very few correct decisions he made as Chancellor, but it was an important one.

Generally, Brown's dominance over economic policy was disastrous. He understood nothing of business and viewed the British economy as an extension of the public sector. He launched a Comprehensive Spending Review to consolidate Treasury control over individual government departments, and was then able to frustrate welfare reform and interfere in defence policy. The NHS was given a great deal of money but no managerial reform, only dozens of targets. The Prime Minister, as First Lord of the Treasury, was often reduced to the role of spectator as his Chancellor kept details of the budgets to himself until the last minute. Brown was therefore able, unconstrained, to build his empire of debt. But this centralization of power in the Treasury did have the one advantage that his opposition to joining the launch of the euro was decisive, overruling the New Labour apparatchiks.

In the same month, the Shadow Cabinet debated the euro. Five members wanted to keep the existing formula of ruling it out in the 'foreseeable future'. The rest, including of course myself, wanted something bolder and more specific, and it was agreed to rule it out for two parliaments, thus committing the party to oppose it at the next election too. So the two main parties were against joining the European single currency, at least for now, thus reversing the position of a few years before when there was almost a national consensus in favour of monetary union. I felt that our campaign had not been in vain. The Liberal Democrats were now alone in championing monetary union. There had been secret negotiations between Labour and the Liberal Democrats before the election about a policy agreement and the possibility of bringing some Lib Dems into the cabinet. These talks continued after the election – part of Blair's vision for a broad left wing coalition – but eventually came to nothing, so that source of euro enthusiasm was stifled.

Blair tried to drive a wedge into the Conservative Party by inviting Conservatives to join a 'patriotic alliance' to prepare for the euro in due course. This achieved some success: in January 1998 a number of 'Tory grandees' signed a letter in the *Independent* highly critical of Conservative policy and strongly supporting the government's position. The signatories, who included Howe, Carrington, Clarke, Heath, Gummer and Patten, were not representative of backbench opinion generally, or the party in the country, but it is always damaging for a party to appear split.

The euro was finally launched without British participation on 1 January 1999, but the preparations had included a renewed drive towards tax harmonization across the EU, and efforts to suppress 'unfair tax competition'. One of these measures threatened the British art market by imposing a levy on the resale of works of art. Under the Droit de Suite (or Artists' Resale Right) a percentage of the sale value would be drawn off every time a work was resold, and paid to the original artist or his heirs, for up to 70 years after his death. France had introduced Droit de Suite in 1920 and eventually eight EU countries adopted a similar levy. The European Commission now wanted to make it compulsory throughout the EU because otherwise art sales could escape the levy by transferring to a country without Droit de Suite, such as the UK. Indeed the British art market had benefited from such sales and was now by far the largest in Europe, employing 51,000 people and attracting many overseas buyers and sellers to London.

There was a glaring flaw in the Commission's argument: by exactly the same logic, any universal EU levy would drive sales out of Europe altogether, to New York, Geneva, Hong Kong or any other centre without Droit de Suite. It beautifully illustrated the inability of the Commission to see Europe in a wider context, or understand the realities of global markets and world competition. The proposals caused great alarm and I wrote a pamphlet, 'A Market Under Threat', published by CPS. In this I was much helped by Anthony Browne, chairman of the British Art Market Federation, who analysed the French experience and found that, instead of helping struggling artists, three-quarters of the levy benefited just six families, including Picasso's estate. The Commission replied to his objections to Droit de Suite with the observation, 'It appears to us that the arguments you put forward reflect to a large extent the views of certain multinational auction houses that are members of your organisation.' In fact Christie's and Sotheby's would not be the main losers as they both had substantial businesses in New York and elsewhere. The victims would be, as always, the small people who could not move: the single dealers, valuers, restorers, and London-based staff. I approached Ken Livingstone, the newly elected Mayor of London, and warned him about the threat to an important industry in the capital and the workers it employed, but he took no interest.

The government, to be fair, understood the threat to a successful British market and resisted the EU Directive. The Prime Minister raised it personally with the French prime minister and the German chancellor, but to no avail. It went through in 2001 by majority voting, another example of EU ideology triumphing over common sense and the wider interests of Europe. The government did salvage something: by special derogation the levy in Britain would apply to living artists only, but in 2011 the coalition government threw in the towel and allowed the derogation to lapse, so the EU legislation now applies in full, to the delight of our overseas competitors.

In 2000 I switched to being Shadow Secretary of State for Trade and Industry. This department had grown much faster than the British economy and was employing a thousand more civil servants than three years before. It had sprouted endless funding initiatives and a suite of Regional Venture Capital Funds which were largely useless. Meanwhile Britain had slid from fourth to ninth in the World Competitiveness League table. I recommended cutting the DTI in half and using the money saved to reduce business rates, to benefit the many not the few, and a version of this was included in our 2001 election manifesto. Other policies fell victim to opposition by focus group. I was told that support for nuclear power would make us appear uncaring, so I was not allowed to raise it, even though there was now a respectable cross-party alliance which saw it as a good way to revive British science and engineering and cut carbon emissions at the same time.

Despite William Hague's manifold political talents, and his stellar performances in the House of Commons, he never shook Blair's popularity lead. Perhaps the job was impossible. At the start of the electoral cycle, an incoming government can survive upsets which at the end of the cycle would bring a tired government down. Before his adventures abroad, and when the feud with Gordon Brown was still manageable, Blair was very difficult to beat.

The election itself was unexciting and the turnout was below 60 per cent, the lowest since 1918. The Conservative vote edged up slightly but this gained us only one seat overall. William Hague resigned immediately. In Wells, I won by 2,796, which was a big improvement on last time but still left me with a marginal seat. The rest of 2001 had bigger shocks in store – later that year both my world, and the world at large, were to be turned upside down.

Chapter 9

Death and its Aftermath

The 2001 leadership election was run under new rules, whereby MPs vote in successive ballots until two candidates remain and they are then voted on by the full party membership. Michael Portillo, who had been Shadow Chancellor since his return to Parliament, seemed to me to be the best modernizing choice and I joined his campaign. Francis Maude, his campaign manager, said they were going for a coronation rather than a contest, which seemed dangerously hubristic. At the post-election party I gave in Wells I thanked everybody and then mentioned I was voting for Portillo, whereupon there was an audible ripple of dissent and even some boos. I had never experienced that from the Wells Association, so something was wrong. Some didn't trust Michael; others felt that he was still on a political journey and hadn't reached his destination, and subsequent events showed there was some truth in this.

Michael Portillo led in the first ballot, ahead of Iain Duncan Smith and Ken Clarke, with Michael Ancram and David Davis eliminated. But Portillo's campaign was losing altitude and when in the next round he slipped to third place, he gave up. So Ken Clarke and Iain Duncan Smith went into a party membership ballot, which IDS won convincingly with 60 per cent of the vote, helped by his record as an effective critic of the EU; however, his lack of support in the parliamentary party as a whole was to be a fatal handicap.

The announcement of the leadership result was delayed by the events of September 11 in the USA. I was visiting a defence contractor in Wells when a shaken secretary came out of an office and told us there had been a massive air attack on New York. I spoke at a school prizegiving in Cheddar that evening and it was already clear that the world had altered. In coordinated suicide attacks, 19 al-Qaeda operatives had piloted the largest flying bombs in history into the World Trade Center and the Pentagon, killing nearly 3,000 people in 45 minutes. The shockwave from that event is still travelling forward in time. It proved the existence of a perverted version of Islam which violently challenged Western values of personal freedom and economic liberation, and it led to an unfocused 'war on terror' and the invasions of Iraq and Afghanistan.

A month before this happened, the world of my family had changed for ever too. It all looked peaceful and secure. Jack, our eldest son, was in his second year at Oxford. Florence, our daughter, was happy at school in London. Matthew had left school and was in his gap year before university. He had always found life more difficult than the others and was often awkward and disorganized, but he conquered his dyslexia at the right time and got a place at Newcastle to read geography. His geography A Level was greatly helped by the fieldwork he did on the effects of glaciation on the Scottish highlands, using the example of a trapped loch near Glenfernate, our place in Scotland. The same year, he completed a round trip across the moors, later written up by a friend, Geoff Rymer, as 'The Legendary Bike Ride'. Surviving a broken chain, a freezing bothy and no food, they crossed rivers and glens and arrived safe home. Geoff wrote, 'Matt was a joy to be with. He was very funny, encouraged me when I was feeling that I couldn't pedal any further and refused to give in when things went wrong. Matt was a dear friend and I count myself lucky to consider myself a friend of his.'

At the start of his gap year Matthew went to Canada to learn high level skiing, but something went wrong and he started to think he was being persecuted or watched in some way. This got better when he was back with us, and for a few months he worked in London restaurants and outside catering, saving money for the trip he really wanted to do, to the Far East. We had some misgivings but he was determined and his confidence had returned. He left for Thailand in June with a friend, Mark Jenkins, and the first letter home was optimistic and full of perception and news. After travelling round

Thailand they crossed into Cambodia and then Vietnam where they went round the Cu Chi tunnels, used by the Viet Cong in what was called the American War, and they also visited a gruesome war museum which seemed to affect Matthew badly. His emails were getting shorter and less frequent and mentioned coming home more often, but on 4 August he was still excited about going to a new part of Vietnam. Then he had a breakdown and lost his passport, but with the help of the British Embassy, Mark got him on a flight home via Bangkok. Matthew's email of 10 August said, 'I have to return. I hope you can pick me up at the airport as I am feeling funny and feeling sad because I miss you loads.' The following day an email from him made no sense and we were now desperately worried.

I flew down from Edinburgh to Heathrow to meet him and when I saw Matthew I hardly recognized him: serious, detached and unresponsive. We flew to Scotland, where I thought the best therapy would be his mother and family, and the place we had spent so many holidays. That afternoon we took him to a doctor in Pitlochry, who referred him to a psychiatrist in Perth. The next morning I drove Matthew to the hospital where he was prescribed an anti-depressant (which we discovered afterwards he failed to take), but he was not taken in as a resident patient because he wanted to come home. We made another appointment for the following day and started for home but his conversation in the car was confused and disconnected, and he seemed to be hearing other voices besides ours. In the afternoon I took him fishing, just the two of us, but my voice was becoming fainter to him. In the evening he seemed to brighten a little and his last words to Linda were, 'I must go and smarten up.' He went to his room and after a little while we were worried and went to look for him. He wasn't in his room and with mounting dread I knew what had happened. There was a gunroom and Matthew must have known where the key was kept. Inside, slumped on a chair, I found him. He had shot himself in the head with a .22 rifle.

An air ambulance took Matthew to Ninewells Hospital in Dundee, while Linda and I and my sister Bridget drove there in a fog of pain and incomprehension. The doctors were professional and candid: there was no saving him, and he was pronounced dead in the early hours of the next morning, 17 August 2001. We entered a pit of blackness and despair. Jack was on his way back from America where he had been doing a holiday job. He had been warned that something was wrong and I had to tell him on the telephone that Matthew was dead, as the news was in the papers and I was afraid he might read the reports before he saw us. Our family, our friends, and Matthew's friends, came to the funeral, held in the small church in the nearby village of Ballintuim. There were several readings, including the matchless lines from Shakespeare's *Romeo and Juliet*:

When he shall die,
Take him and cut him out in little stars,
And he will make the face of heaven so fine
That all the world will be in love with night,
And pay no worship to the garish sun.

Florence read from Alexander Solzhenitsyn's poem:

Some people are bound to die young.
By dying young, a person stays young forever
in people's memory.
If he burns brightly before he dies,
his light shines for all time.

That is certainly true for me: there is not a day since then that I haven't thought of Matthew in some way.

At the end of the service, as the coffin was carried out, a friend pushed the button on a CD player and we heard 'Sand Dunes' by Groove Armada, which Matthew often played in happier times. He was buried in Kirkmichael graveyard, on the edge of the village with a view of the hills. The following year we commissioned a slate headstone with Matthew's name and dates, and a line from Philip Larkin ('An Arundel Tomb'), 'What will survive of us is love'.

As we left the graveyard, leaving him in the damp earth, it seemed our whole existence had collapsed. The world is full of trials and disappointments, but happiness can be found in the small crucible of the family, and now that was shattered. I knew that Linda had been the best mother imaginable but she was inconsolable, wracked by remorse and guilt. What had gone wrong and could we have saved Matthew?

We believed wrongly that the love and care we could give him at home would cure him from whatever had afflicted him on his travels. We will never know the demons that drove him back or what went on in his head in these last fateful days. Certainly the Matthew we knew never came home. We sorted out his few pathetic possessions and the contents of his knapsack. There was no note or clue. The consultant in the Perth hospital whom we saw the next day said, 'he died of an illness', and gave us his opinion that Matthew would have found some other way to take his life, but I had underestimated the severity of that illness.

Many people wrote to us, friends, constituents, and parliamentary colleagues from all sides. Geoffrey Robinson sent a kind note, which was especially generous. These letters were a great help, although people meeting us personally often didn't know how to react or what to say. With modern medicine we think we have conquered death, so when it happens suddenly, particularly to a child, all our defences are down. But we were not alone. Those who lose children enter a community of the bereft. We had many meetings with those who had suffered in the same way, and we set up a charity in Matthew's name, with the dual objects of promoting outdoor activities for young people in trouble, and also the prevention of suicide, which, after traffic accidents, is the second commonest cause of death in young people, particularly boys. The wound of Matthew's death will never really heal, but at least we had him for 19 years, and no life is ever wasted. The saddest moments today are when we visit places where we were all together, but Matthew is no longer by my side.

Iain Duncan Smith, confirmed as the new Conservative leader, offered me a shadow cabinet job but I had to come to terms with what had just happened, so I thanked him and said no. But I had to keep working, and at the end of the year a job came up which seemed right for me, even if it meant travelling to Brussels every week.

Chapter 10

Left at the Crossroads

By 2001, it was obvious that something was wrong with the European Union. There was a growing disconnection between the way the EU did business and the wishes of ordinary voters. Turnout in elections to the European Parliament had fallen steadily in almost every country, and was now below 50 per cent. When the public weren't indifferent, they were hostile. The Danes had recently voted no to joining the single currency and Ireland had just rejected the Nice Treaty in a referendum.

In December 2001, the EU heads of government meeting in Laeken in Belgium issued a Declaration which was, by their diplomatic standards, candid about the failings. The EU was, 'behaving too bureaucratically' and, 'the European institutions must be brought closer to the citizens'. It portentously declared that, 'the Union stands at a crossroads, a defining moment in its existence', and it proposed a solution. A Convention on the Future of Europe would be held to define the respective powers of the Union and member states, to simplify the rules and create, 'more democracy, transparency and efficiency'. It was even suggested that some powers should be returned to member states. The convention would be chaired by Valéry Giscard d'Estaing, a former President of France, and would be attended by ministers from each state, and representatives from national parliaments, the European Parliament and the Commission – 105 delegates in all.

The question arose, who would fill the two places allocated to the UK Parliament? The Labour Party appointed Gisela Stuart, German born and now a British MP. The Conservative nomination was more complicated because three of us applied: John Maples, Patrick

Cormack and myself. An election was held which I won, and after formal approval by the House of Commons I was on my way again to Brussels.

The Convention on the Future of Europe opened to applause in the vast European Parliament building on 28 February 2002. The *Guardian* enthused that, 'The Philadelphia Convention of 1787 defined America; now the EU could be on the brink of a new existence'. Chairman Giscard d'Estaing took the comparison with America further, and likened himself to Thomas Jefferson, until it was pointed out that Jefferson was abroad at the time of the Philadelphia Convention and was anyway a strong supporter of states' rights. I tried not to be cynical. Maybe this time the voice of the public would break through. The evidence for the EU's 'democratic deficit' was undeniable. That is what the Laeken Declaration said. We were at a crossroads, so presumably we had a choice about which road to take.

After the opening ceremony, the members (and a similar number of alternates who could attend and speak in our absence), milled about in the foyer like a huge cocktail party without drinks. Not all of them looked lost: the MEPs and Commission members were on home territory and this gave them an advantage. The secretariat too was drawn exclusively from full-time EU staff, Brussels insiders whose careers were entirely bound up with the central institutions. Chairman Giscard, himself one of the architects of the EU, was flanked by two vice-chairman, both ex-prime ministers. Jean-Luc Dehaene (vetoed as Commission president by John Major for being too federalist) supposedly represented the centre-right. Giuliano Amato, one of the innumerable ex-prime ministers of Italy, was of the left. They made a strange trio on the podium: Giscard, tall and hawklike; Dehaene, large and Buddha shaped; Amato, like a quizzical chipmunk. But they knew what they wanted, and to achieve it they appointed as Secretary General, Sir John Kerr, whose legendary drafting skills were now to be deployed in writing a constitution.

In searching for allies, I started with two groups which regularly met before the main Convention sessions. One was composed of all the national MPs present and was supposed to ensure that the interests of national parliaments were protected, and to call a halt to the endless transfer of powers upwards to the EU. Reflecting our tourist status in the Convention, these meetings were chaotically run and completely unfocused. By contrast, the European Parliament members, who also met as a group, were clear in their aim – more powers for their parliament – and worked tirelessly to secure it. The suggestion in the Laeken Declaration that some powers should be returned to national parliaments was buried.

The other group I belonged to was the European Peoples Party (EPP), the centre-right grouping which the Conservative Party was part of. Like its mirror image, the European Socialist Party, the EPP was entirely federalist in its outlook and ambitions. The chairman, a burly German MEP called Elmar Brok, later produced a fully worked-up constitutional text for the EU, which he tried to present as an EPP document. It was actually more centralizing than the one eventually adopted by the Convention. I wrote to Brok disowning his constitution and asking instead that the efforts of the EPP Group be directed at reconnecting to the public. I also suggested that we should study why Europe suffered from low growth and high unemployment, since without a better economic future the EU would have no political future. These suggestions were ignored and it remained a mystery why the Conservative Party was allied to a political grouping whose beliefs we did not share. Seven years later, the Conservative MEPs left the EPP and formed a new group, European Conservatives and Reformists, and thereby struck a blow for honest representation.

By now I had found some allies in the Convention. Jens-Peter Bonde was an MEP and leader of the June Movement in Denmark, which supported EU membership but believed it should only deal with cross-border issues such as trade. We founded the Democracy Forum, which never had more than nine members but was a crucial resistance group to the prevailing orthodoxy of the Convention. It was a rainbow coalition, from six countries including France and the Czech Republic, and from seven political parties including the Left Party in Finland, the Irish Greens, and the Danish People's Party. The common factor was a belief in democratic reform, and the search for a people's Europe, rather than a politician's Europe. Ten countries from Eastern Europe were participating in the Convention even though they were not yet members of the EU, but their representatives were disappointingly reticent about standing up for themselves, perhaps because they were shy of crossing the European Commission with whom they were negotiating their terms of entry. Also, many of them were in line for EU jobs, as commissioners or MEPs, and had already caught the EU bug. The exception was Jan Zahradil, a Czech MP from the successful Civic Democrat Party, who stuck with us to the end despite criticism at home and arranged for me to address his party's national convention in Prague. He eventually became chairman of the European Conservatives and Reformists. I resigned from the EPP Group and from then on based myself in Bonde's office on the eighth floor of the parliament building, where we met before each session of the Convention to plan tactics and table amendments.

The presidency held regular press conferences at which Giscard would give an Olympian account of progress in the Convention. The Democracy Forum always booked the following slot in the press room and, after Giscard and most of the press corps filed out, we held our own press conference. The room was seldom full but in June we scored our first hit. A Civic Forum had been held to get the wider views of outside bodies and NGOs. It turned out that almost all the chosen participants were associated with the EU and usually received funding from the EU budget. Thus, the European Women's Lobby and the European Environmental Bureau were hardly likely to be critical of the body that was paying them. Before the session started, I raised a point of order to require each organization to declare any financial dependency, but this was refused without discussion. At the Democracy Forum press conference afterwards we published the full list, under the heading 'Brussels talking to

Brussels', which was then taken up by the press because the activities of lobby groups, and the revolving-door nature of much EU business, was already attracting criticism.

A month later, a three-day Youth Convention was held, attended by 210 young people drawn from all member states. I made an agreement with Peter Hain, the British government representative on the Convention, that our youth members should be chosen by a panel after advertising the opportunity in a national newspaper. Hain broke that promise, although I managed to ensure that at least one of our participants reflected the majority view, from young and old, that European integration had gone far enough. In the event, 51 of the youth members signed a statement saying the Youth Convention had been, 'conducted in a manner that was unrepresentative, undemocratic and too concerned with vested interests and political factions'. This experiment with outside participation was judged a failure and was not repeated.

It was clear by now that the main Convention was in the business of drafting a European Constitution. The Laeken Declaration, which set up the Convention, did not include this amongst its tasks. The only reference to a constitution was tentative: 'The question ultimately arises whether this simplification and reorganisation might not lead in the long run to the adoption of a constitutional text in the Union.' So the Convention was already picking out those tasks which it wanted and ignoring the others. This was not welcomed by the British government which saw that the UK would thereby be getting a written constitution for the first time, but they gave in without a struggle, the first of many such retreats.

Nor was the case for a European constitution ever debated, although I tried to question it. The comparison with America could have been instructive, and in order not to appear too Anglo Saxon in my criticism I brought up the name of a French aristocrat, Alexis de Tocqueville, who visited America in 1831 and analysed the vigour and success of the American federal system in a famous book, *Democracy in America*. De Tocqueville realized that the system rested on a number of preconditions, including a common language, a habit of self-government and a set of shared moral values amongst the governing class. Crucially, he saw that the American Constitution was not just a legally enforceable document, but depended for its success on the 'manners and customs' of the people.

In Europe, the pattern of loyalties and allegiances is different and is centred on the nation state. These countries are varied and diverse, reflecting widely different historical experiences. Some have a continental character, while others, like Britain, have a maritime tradition and instinctively look outwards to the wider world. This has led to differences in legal traditions, and attitudes towards the role of the state and the origin of rights. There is no European People, no single electorate or coherent public opinion. In short, there is no European *demos* on which to found a supranational democracy or federation. Nor can such a *demos* be created by artificial means such as an EU flag, an anthem, a 'Europe day' or any number of EU information campaigns. Identity is not bestowed by government; it flows upwards from the people. As de Tocqueville observed, these things lie in the manners and customs of the people and are the product of history and shared experience, not of bureaucratic engineering.

The underlying problem for the Convention was that Europe, and especially the EU, lacked a popular identity. People need a sense of identity and belonging and they do not find this in supranational institutions. The natural focus for people's loyalties and affections is the nation state, through familiarity, language and history. This makes self-government possible, as people agree to obey laws which they can control through the democratic process. This is impossible in remote bodies like the EU. They may take on the trappings of statehood, with flags, laws and parliaments, but they can never pass the democratic test. Giving the European Parliament more powers, in the hope that people would then respect it, was a failure. Successive treaty changes had already given the European Parliament more power, but turnout in those elections continued to fall because people did not feel represented in any real way in this institution whose proceedings they could not understand, and whose composition they could scarcely influence. In the words of a French MP who came to our Democracy Forum meetings, we were building 'a Europe without the people, an offshore state without legitimacy or efficiency'.

The 2002 World Cup was being played during the early months of the Convention and provided a reminder of where popular enthusiasm lay. Football is a huge global enterprise, with players traded freely around the world, but it is rooted in people's loyalty to national teams. The patriotic fervour of the world cup games found no understanding in the proceedings of the Convention, where the public was kept at a safe distance. At this stage the Convention members had no inkling that eventually their product would have to face the judgement of the people in national referendums, with disagreeable results.

On my weekly journeys by Eurostar I started to recognize some of my fellow travellers. These were the Brussels regulars, representing large companies or trade bodies, going to the EU to sit on committees or draft new regulations. Big business likes big government, and the corporatist culture of the EU institutions was very congenial. I never met anyone in Brussels from a small business, yet it was they who had to bear the brunt of the regulations.

Before each meeting of the Convention I usually got up early to run round the city, as I was preparing for the London Marathon. I had run the race 15 years before and wanted to beat my time of just under 4 hours and also raise money for the National Blind Children's Society, which was based in my constituency. Apart from a few tourist areas like the Grande Place, Brussels was not a very inspiring city, perhaps because it was also a divided one, split between hostile blocs of French and Flemish speakers, and often without a functioning national government. The parks were particularly disappointing, so I generally kept to the small streets and squares in my outings at dawn.

On 14 April I set off with 33,000 other runners from Greenwich on this most exhilarating of all mass events. There had been one welcome development since 1987. Then, starting near the back, I ran for a good few minutes before passing a large sign that said, 'Start'. This time, we had tiny transponders to fit on our shoes which were activated when we went over the starting line, so our time was accurately measured. As before, the assorted rhino-suit wearers, running chickens, spidermen, daleks and deep-sea divers started to thin out after 10 miles, but I fell in with an excellent Elvis Presley impersonator for the middle part of the race, until he overheated inside his suit. Finally, Big Ben came into view and then the Mall and the finishing line, after 3 hours 58 minutes, which was 3 minutes slower than my 1987 time; but 15 years of House of Commons food and drink is bound to have some effect. The morning after the race my legs were so stiff I had to go downstairs on my bottom. I made it to Brussels on the early train and joined in the Convention, where Chairman Giscard, ever well briefed and charming, congratulated me during the first session and suggested that I spoke sitting down.

The Convention next moved from a supposed 'listening phase' to a 'study phase', and a number of working groups were set up on matters such as legal powers, simplification, external action (foreign policy), defence, and the role of national parliaments. I served on one with the title of 'Complementary Competences', itself a baffling piece of eurospeak which showed the EU's inability to explain itself in normal language. 'Competences' meant 'powers' and this working group was supposed to draw a clearer distinction between the powers of member states and those of the EU; in other words, 'who does what'. The group did at least allow some discussion, unlike the main sessions of the Convention where speaking time was limited to three minutes (later reduced to two). It was chaired by an agreeable Dane, Henning Christophersen, and by chance the composition of the group was comparatively hostile to giving more powers to the EU, so here was an opportunity to challenge the prevailing mindset.

As I had discovered before when in the Foreign Office, German politicians would never challenge the basic mission of the EU as they felt that Germany was only tolerable to its neighbours when firmly tied in to a supranational structure. However they were helpful over matters such as trade and the importance of the

American connection, and with very few exceptions I found them friendly and cooperative. But they had a weakness for rules, however unrealistic or unenforceable. For instance, they seemed to believe that the euro would work because the Stability and Growth Pact had put limits on national borrowing. This was somewhat undermined when both Germany and France were both found to have breached the borrowing limit, but no sanctions were applied. The important thing was to have rules even if they were disobeyed.

The French were cynical about rules, but they were much better on the big question of statehood, and they wanted to keep the Council of Ministers and national governments in overall change. They were scornful of the European Parliament, which they saw as a legislature but not a real parliament. But below the surface there was a deep pool of suspicion and resentment about the English-speaking world. I found that they would rarely cooperate with us and their overriding concern was to manage the Germans. The Italian delegation included some members of the Northern League who were very robust in private, but hopelessly unreliable as allies and often didn't turn up.

Nevertheless, I found some allies on the working group, particularly among the Germans, who wanted to protect the rights of their Länder over matters such as education. The final report of our working group was very unwelcome to the European Commission and most of the European Parliament members. We recommended abolishing the EU Treaty commitment to 'an ever closer union', since this was an invitation to the EU to keep the escalator going. We wanted the opaque 'complementary competences' to be redefined as 'supporting measures', to make clear that the primary power should rest with member states. And we recommended radical reform of the notorious 'rubber article', number 308 in the Treaty, by which the EU could extend its powers into new policy areas without treaty amendment. These modest proposals were denounced as major heresies when debated in the full Convention. It was even suggested that chairman Christophersen had allowed his own Danish assistant to draft the report rather than handing this crucial task to the

Convention secretariat, which of course would have strangled these ideas at birth. As it was, not one of our proposals survived into the final text of the Convention. Instead a large number of policies, such as transport, energy, the environment, and justice and home affairs, were declared to be 'shared competences'. This was defined to mean that if the EU decided to legislate on such areas, member states would be forbidden to do so, which was an odd definition of sharing. It certainly confused rather than clarified the question of 'who does what'. It was dispiriting to see all the effort we had put into the working group smothered in this way.

Any idea that the Convention was a bottom-up exercise, driven by ordinary convention members, was rapidly evaporating. Gisela Stuart, my co-member from the House of Commons, was on the Praesidium, the 13-strong committee chaired by Chairman Giscard which was supposed to guide the proceedings and shape the out-come. She later wrote a pamphlet, 'The Making of Europe's Constitution', describing her experience:

> The Convention brought together a self-selected group of the European political elite, many of who have their eyes on a career at European level, which is dependent on more and more integration and who see national governments and national parliaments as an obstacle. Not once in the sixteen months I spent in the Convention did representatives question whether deeper integration is what the people of Europe want.

Her comments on the working methods were also revealing:

> The Praesidium was the drafting body, deciding which working groups' recommendations should be accepted almost un-changed and which should be almost ignored ... The secretariat was very skilful when it came to deciding which decisions of the Praesidium would be reflected in subsequent papers.

Coming from an avowedly pro-European position, Gisela Stuart ended up as disillusioned as I was with the predetermined outcome of the Convention.

In October 2002 we all received copies of a draft European Constitution. It was never clear where it came from or who had drafted it, but from then on it was the basic document on which the Convention worked. The first part set out the objectives of the Union, which was now given its own legal personality and given explicit 'primacy over the law of the Member States'. A new full-time President of the European Council was proposed, together with a Minister for Foreign Affairs – both of them unelected of course. Then there were more than 100 pages which repeated, and occasionally strengthened, all the articles in the existing EU treaties. This was because, under the doctrine of the 'occupied field', no powers could be relinquished, only added to. So all the obscurity and legalese in the existing texts was being carried into the new constitution. We were building a Europe for lawyers. The instruction in the Laeken Declaration to produce a document accessible to ordinary people was simply ignored.

We were free to table amendments to the constitution and I put down nearly a thousand, greatly helped by Dr Lee Rotherham, my research assistant, whose political savvy and knowledge of the treaties were indispensable. Amendments were grouped together and discussed, but never voted on as we were supposed to advance 'by consensus'. Peter Hain tabled more than 200 amendments on behalf of the British government, but only 11 were accepted. We occasionally met as a British delegation and on some issues there was an identifiable national position which we could all support. I offered to be the last man standing if a row was needed, but neither Peter Hain nor his alternate, Lady Scotland, showed any interest in working with us, so that opportunity was missed.

Nor were the government's acolytes any better. Digby Jones (later a Labour peer) was Director General of the CBI and should have been interested in the danger of over-regulation. The draft constitution included new EU powers over economic and employment policies, and also brought in majority voting to 36 new areas, which meant the end of national blocking powers. I wrote to Digby Jones offering to raise any concerns he had, and suggesting that the CBI should ask the Convention to defend European competitiveness. I got an acknowledgement from his secretary but no reply, and nothing was done. He later complained publicly that the House of Commons was, 'asleep on the job', in resisting red tape and excessive regulation, but he was fast asleep during the Convention on the Future of Europe.

The government was certainly worried about the creation of an EU foreign minister who would 'conduct the Union's common foreign and security policy', through an 'external action service'. Peter Hain tried unsuccessfully to delete the requirement that the UK, as a member of the UN Security Council, would have to offer up its seat to the EU foreign minister when discussing matters of common interest. Towards the end of the Convention I was contacted by FCO officials trying to coordinate resistance to some of these encroachments, but it was too late. Tony Blair's much vaunted 'influence through engagement', was no match for the determination of the EU insiders to move to the next stage of European integration.

The other area where an intergovernmental structure was dismantled and replaced by EU policy making was justice and home affairs. A working group under the chairmanship of John Bruton, former prime minister of Ireland, was set up to examine this and John Kerr asked me to serve on it, supposedly as a counterweight to the centralizing tendency. This proved an impossible task. Their opening bid, circulated as a 'first draft', was for many crimes, penalties and criminal procedures to be standardized across the EU by majority voting. I warned that this was a very sensitive area, which went to the core of what a nation state is for. The coercive power of the state to punish and imprison, or to decide on immigration, raised vital questions of accountability and control. It was also dangerous to merge the distinctive English and Scottish legal systems with the different inquisitorial system found on the Continent.

The key argument was one of democracy. If important decisions about immigration, asylum and criminal justice were moved away from member states upwards to the EU, it made it impossible for voters to make real choices in general elections. Parties offering to change things at election time must possess the powers to do so otherwise they are making false promises. Already, too many such decisions had been transferred to an opaque and unresponsive European government and this had created the feelings of distrust and alienation identified in the Laeken Declaration. That is why Laeken called for a Europe, 'closer to its citizens'. Yet the Convention was proposing to move decisions even further away from the citizen, to the most remote tier of government of all, the EU. It was, again, not just ignoring the Laeken instructions but defying them.

Since votes were impossible, I could only ask that my objections be recorded, but the final report of the Justice and Home Affairs working group more or less ignored dissident opinions. Remarkably, the articles written into the European Constitution went even further than the working group recommendations, and included plans for a European Public Prosecutor who would launch criminal prosecutions across member states. Although this could only be set up by unanimous vote of all states, it was a pointer to the future and a statement of intent. As well as the 'occupied field' the Commission always looked for a 'foot in the door'. The British government objected and Peter Hain put down some amendments to delete the European Public Prosecutor, but he was overridden.

The next matter to exercise the Convention was human rights. All member states were already signed up to the 1950 European Convention on Human Rights (ECHR) based at Strasbourg. However the EU wanted its own bill of rights, so in 2000 it had drawn up a separate Charter of Fundamental Rights, which would apply to member states when they were implementing Community law. This duplicated many of the articles in the ECHR but used slightly different language, which would create difficulty as the case law of each started to diverge. Also, the rights in the charter went further than the ECHR and included a number of open-ended rights such as universal access to health care, social security and housing assistance, and guaranteed environmental and consumer protection, which are matters for governments and very difficult to define judicially.

The Convention could have been the occasion for an overdue debate about the role and scope of human rights legislation. Originally designed to protect 'hard rights' such as the right to a fair trial, freedom from persecution and freedom of speech, these rights had steadily multiplied and were now used to advance 'soft rights' like equal pay and access to housing. These were encroaching on matters of political choice, best left to elected governments rather than foreign judges, and were creating a huge backlog of cases. No such debate took place, as it might have undermined the steady advance of EU jurisdiction.

The government was right to be worried by the prospect of the Charter of Fundamental Rights becoming part of the European Constitution and thus gaining the status of treaty law. They had only agreed to the charter in 2000 on the basis that it would be a source of guidance and inspiration, and was not legally binding. That was the assurance given to Parliament by Lord Goldsmith, the Attorney General. Keith Vaz, the Europe Minister, claimed that the charter would have no more legal effect than a copy of the *Beano*. Such reckless assurances were often the prelude to a climbdown, and so it proved. The whole text of the Charter of Fundamental Rights was incorporated into the European Constitution and given explicit legal effect. And since the Constitution was to be given, 'primacy over the law of the member states', that meant that the charter, as interpreted by the European Court of Justice, would automatically override parliament. The European Court set no limit on its own powers, and, being itself an EU institution, was not an impartial arbiter between the rights of member states and the rights of the EU.

Towards the end of 2002 the tempo increased when France and Germany appointed their foreign ministers to the Convention. They jointly advocated more powers for the European Commission and the European Parliament, and the creation of a new full-time President of the Council. The Convention had already become a forum for institutional bargaining, resulting in more powers for everyone. As the Dodo said in *Alice in Wonderland* when asked who had won the Caucus race, 'Everybody has won, and all must have prizes'.

At a breakfast meeting with Romano Prodi, the President of the Commission, in his Europe-sized office, I asked him how the task of making the EU more democratic could be squared with giving even more power to the unelected Commission, which sat at the apex of bureaucratic Europe. He replied that, 'the Commission has just as much democratic legitimacy as any member state government'. I have no idea whether he believed this nonsense; he was certainly one of the least impressive men in a senior position whom I ever met.

The only institutions to get no prizes in this new share out of powers were national parliaments. The scrap thrown to them was an idea that they should have a bigger role in policing 'subsidiarity', which was the principle that the EU should not interfere in matters better dealt with at member state level. It was proposed that, if a group of national parliaments objected to an EU law on the grounds that it broke the subsidiarity rule, it would be referred back to the European Commission. The Commission would then look at it again, but could still proceed, so national parliaments were simply getting a new right to be ignored. The all-party European Scrutiny Committee observed, 'There is no requirement for any of the EU institutions to take the slightest notice.' There was something pathetic about the eagerness with which Labour ministers nevertheless tried to sell this to the House of Commons as a great step forward in reasserting democratic control over the EU.

These developments extinguished any hope of making the EU more democratic and accessible to ordinary voters, so I resigned myself to total opposition. I got a pained note from John Kerr after one critical intervention, saying that he and Giscard were trying to restrain the more extreme centralizers and needed allies. It was too late for that. The whole Convention was biased against genuine enquiry or any alternative to the 'Community Method'.

By coincidence I was mugged shortly after this, in the street when I was returning late one evening to my hotel. A hooded man with a knife appeared from the shadows and demanded my briefcase, which I handed over. He ran off but I followed, shouting, 'Arrêtez le voleur!' Having some vestigial fitness from my marathon race, I began to gain on him. Windows in the street started to open and a Belgian bicyclist joined the chase. Eventually the assailant dropped my case and ran off, so he never had the chance to read my speech notes.

As the Convention was becoming empty of debate, I pursued other outlets. I contributed a weekly article to a website, EU Observer, and spoke at conferences in Denmark, Estonia, France, Austria and the Czech Republic. To keep the House of Commons informed a joint committee of Lords and Commons had been formed, at which Gisela Stuart and myself spoke and answered questions. Then there were the normal debates in the House where Jack Straw as Foreign Secretary defended the government's position, and I sometimes detected a lack of personal conviction in some of the bland assurances he had to give. We also visited Scotland, Wales and Northern Ireland to warn the devolved assemblies that the European Constitution was a kind of reverse devolution, whereby powers would be passed upwards to the EU, not downwards to them. It was baffling that the Scottish and Welsh national parties, so determined to take powers back from the British government, were apparently willing to hand them over to the EU.

I and other members of the Democracy Forum started to agitate for a referendum on the outcome of the Convention. In early 2003 a petition calling for national referendums circulated in the Convention and attracted nearly a hundred signatures. This caused consternation in the EU high command because they had seen the results of the referendums in Ireland and Denmark. They argued that the European Constitution would be too complicated for people to understand. But that was the fault of the drafters: they had been instructed to simplify the EU treaties but we had ended up with a 300-page text which was actually longer than what it replaced. Their draft started with the words, 'Reflecting the will of the citizens and states of Europe to build a common future', so it was difficult for them to argue that the citizens should not be consulted. The British government was adamantly against a referendum. The new Europe Minister, Denis MacShane, called it, 'an opportunity for populists', which was a revealing objection. Peter Hain said that campaigners, 'should put away their placards because there isn't going to be a referendum'. This from the man who had dug up cricket pitches in the anti-apartheid campaign but was now determined to stop people having a say on how they were governed. These denials made the government's later U-turn all the more spectacular.

Negotiations on the text continued right up to the end, but on Friday, 13 June 2003, Giscard announced that the Convention had a product, a European Constitution, which would be presented to member states at their next meeting in Greece. His speech was followed by much self-congratulation by Convention members, and then the hall filled with the strains of Beethoven's Ode to Joy and glasses of champagne were handed out. Poor Beethoven, I thought; he hated pomposity and humbug but had no control over this endorsement. The only discordant voice was Jens-Peter Bonde from our Democracy Forum, who held his ground and announced that eight of us would be presenting a minority report. Titled, 'A Europe of Democracies', this called for, 'a treaty association of free and self-governing European states and an open economic area.' This would rest on the secure foundations of national parliamentary democracy. The European Commission would lose its monopoly right to initiate legislation and instead would become the secretariat to national parliaments, which would come together to tackle cross-frontier issues where states could not effectively act alone. Simplified voting rights were laid down. The legal activism of the European Court was curbed, and all meetings and documents would be open to the public. Our minority report ran to four pages and we thought it admirably fulfilled the Laeken mandate of democracy, brevity, clarity and efficiency. John Kerr assured me it would be presented to the European Council meeting. It lies alongside the European

Constitution in an archive vault in Rome, forgotten but not discredited.

Despite our show of defiance, Giscard claimed that the draft European Constitution had been agreed, 'by consensus'. The European Council meeting in Greece accepted it was a 'good basis' for an intergovernmental conference to be held later in the year. This was widely expected to endorse the Constitution, which would then be ratified by member states and pass into law. It was the voters who were to upset this orderly train of events.

Chapter 11

The Unexpected
Happens Again

At home, the troubled leadership of Iain Duncan Smith was drawing to a close – 25 Conservative MPs were required to trigger a motion of no confidence and I was one of them. The Conservative Party is much more brutal about this than Labour, who struggle on with failing leaders long after this has become obvious. Iain lost the subsequent vote and Michael Howard, who had done well as Shadow Chancellor, was elected unopposed in November 2003.

The Iraq war had begun in March and I had very nearly voted against it, believing that British interests were not sufficiently engaged and that violent Islam was better countered in other ways. There was a messianic quality about Tony Blair which saw the world as divided into good and evil, but this was not always a sound guide for foreign policy. But I voted for the war, for two not very good reasons. First, I was already being a nuisance over Europe, which took up a lot of my time, and there was a general rule that one rebellion at a time was enough. Second, I wrongly thought that if a British prime minister stands at the dispatch box and tells the House of Commons about a lethal threat from Weapons of Mass Destruction, that should be true and sufficient. But it was not true and not sufficient and there is no doubt that Tony Blair misled us, based on reckless intelligence that was biased in favour of finding what it looked for.

After the end of the Convention on the Future of Europe I wrote a pamphlet on the subject, published by CPS, which explained in layman's terms what was at stake and why a referendum was essential, and a well-wisher paid for a reprint to be sent free to magazine subscribers. I visited the United States to speak at a Heritage Foundation conference on Europe, and took the opportunity to lobby the government there on the threat to American interests if European foreign policy became centred on Brussels. I saw John Bolton in the State Department, and Robert Zoellick, US Trade Representative, but it was clear that, for George Bush, the support of Tony Blair over Iraq was all that mattered, and if Blair supported the European Constitution, so would he.

It was a relief not to be getting the early train to Brussels every week and I reverted to a more normal parliamentary life. I had time for other campaigns and I was pleased to win a Charity Champion award for helping blind people. I also joined the Treasury select committee in order to pick up the threads of domestic policy. It was a sobering experience, looking at the national accounts again, and seeing the relentless growth in the size of the state, the complexity of the tax system and the miles of red tape. It all rested on the fallacy of endless economic growth and cost-free borrowing, but no one was predicting how it would all end. Gordon Brown's central political belief was in the superiority of the public sector and that it was the task of everybody else to supply it with more cash every year. In appearing before the Treasury select committee he showed impressive command of detail, but was pathologically incapable of taking criticism of any kind, which meant he was a very grumpy witness and must have been an impossible parliamentary colleague.

The European question lay quiet for several months and then flared up again as it always did. The intergovernmental conference which was considering the draft constitution was deadlocked by Spain and Poland over voting rights, but this was eventually resolved. The European Constitution which they finally agreed differed very little from the one we had laboured over for 15 months. The next stage was legal ratification by all member states, which now numbered 25, as the 10 East European countries had joined in May 2004.

Then, quite suddenly, Tony Blair announced that a UK referendum would be held after all. In a statement to the House, he described the importance of what was at stake and the need to decide on the whole future of the EU, but he still couldn't bring himself to utter the word 'referendum'. To hoots of derision he ended up by saying, 'let the people have the final say'. Only three weeks before, all Labour MPs had filed obediently through the division lobby against a Conservative motion calling for a referendum, and ministers had emphatically and repeatedly ruled one out. What had changed Blair's mind? Electoral considerations. Jack Straw, who privately never liked the European Constitution, persuaded the Prime Minister that the campaign for a referendum was taking off, and Labour could not go into a general election the following year as the only party that denied people a vote on something so important. This was the party that had held referendums in Northern Ireland, Scotland and Wales, as well as in London and 30 other cities to decide if they should have elected mayors.

For me, it was the culmination of two years' campaigning, or what was later called, 'banging on about Europe'. Peter Hain, for the government, had spent months claiming it was just a 'tidying up exercise', but it was plainly entitled, 'A Treaty establishing a Constitution for Europe.' This meant that member states were having their powers defined and limited as well. So Britain was getting a written constitution for the first time since Oliver Cromwell signed the short-lived Articles of Government in 1653. I was clear on the merits of representative democracy and the sparing use of direct referendums. But when the rules of government change they must be agreed by popular vote. That was the point made by Tom Paine in *The Rights of Man*: 'A constitution is not the act of a government, but of a people.'

Not all the campaigning was quite so high minded. The *Sun* had developed a robust attitude towards Europe, and had greeted Jacques Delors with the headline, 'Up Yours Delors', inviting him to, 'Frog Off!' I met the editor, Rebekah Wade, at a Conservative party conference and agreed to turn my pamphlet into a *Sun* publication, to be distributed free to every reader. The result was, 'Shackle Britain – Europe's secret plan. Inside: The full shock story'. I helped them with the text and was incredibly impressed by their skill in turning complex ideas into political punch points. The 18-page booklet covered everything: the economy and the pound, defence, foreign policy, immigration, and justice, and had boxes contrasting 'Eurospeak' with ' Plain English From The Sun.' Its conclusion was simple: 'The Sun says, Give us a vote.'

EU enthusiasts sometimes complained that the unpopularity of their creation was all the fault of the 'eurosceptic press'. In fact, for many years euroscepticism remained a fringe activity and it was only slowly that the tabloids developed an appetite for reporting some of the grosser abuses. Even then, the mainstream press remained generally sympathetic to European integration. The *Financial Times* enthusiastically advocated every ill-fated EU project, from entry to the ERM to joining the euro. The same was true of business organizations: only the Institute of Directors and the Federation of Small Businesses held out against the prevailing orthodoxy. The CBI, under a succession of compliant presidents and directors-general, supported the European Constitution and the principle of monetary union, repeating the government line that it was all about 'stability' and 'influence' and 'being at the top table'.

Tony Blair's rubber-burning U-turn on the referendum put pressure on others, and three months later Jacques Chirac announced that France too would hold a referendum the following year. From then on the European Constitution was doomed. The yes campaign in France started with a 2 to 1 lead but this gradually dissolved. The government sent everyone a copy of the Constitution, but when 200 pages of impenetrable Eurojargon thumped on to the doormats of 40 million French voters it only increased their alarm. On 29 May 2005, France voted 55:45 against ratifying the European Constitution, on a high turnout. Three days later, Holland voted against even more convincingly, 61:39. This was a shattering result. When small or new countries voted no, they were regularly ignored. But such decisive votes from France and Holland, two founder members of the EU, could not be dismissed so easily. A 'period of reflection' was announced so that the EU could find a way round the obstacle of public opinion.

Meanwhile, there had been a general election here, with Blair winning an unprecedented third term for Labour. Michael Howard was unable to capitalize on the unpopularity of the Iraq war, or the evident failure to plan it properly, because the party had backed it at the start. Blair and Brown had temporarily suspended their running feud over who should be prime minister, although even if only half of the subsequent memoirs are true, we had a Chancellor of the Exchequer who was frankly deranged. In public, Gordon Brown was relentlessly hostile to opposition spokesmen, but there was another side to him. I was leaving the House of Commons late one evening and saw him talking to Gus O'Donnell, permanent secretary to the Treasury, whom I knew when he was John Major's press secretary. I went over to them and Gordon Brown was completely charming, referred approvingly to my work on the Treasury select committee, and wished me well. He was incapable of showing this persona to the public, who saw only the hard carapace and the jaw-jerking verbal delivery. However, the longsuffering British economy was still delivering the goods for the government to spend, and the essential tax-and-spend doctrine of New Labour was yet to be exposed.

In the 2005 election, Labour's vote fell to 35 per cent of the votes cast, but the Conservatives only won 33 more seats, with the Liberal Democrats gaining 11. In Somerset it was the usual mixture, with us getting Weston-super-Mare back from the Lib Dems, but losing Taunton. My majority crept up to just over 3,000. Michael Howard immediately announced he would be standing down, but would stay on until a new leader was elected, perhaps under new rules. He formed a new shadow team and asked me to join Work and Pensions under Malcolm Rifkind, who had just been elected for a London seat. Being an opposition spokesman is a much overrated occupation, but I accepted and for seven months dealt with the social security system and policies for the disabled. I learned a good deal about the daily struggles, the overlooked hurdles and the precarious lives of many disabled people, and I organized a number of conferences for them and their representatives. Some were unreasonable and impossible to deal with, but most were realistic as well as determined, and very helpful in working to design a better system in which benefits are not a way of life.

David Blunkett was Secretary of State for Work and Pensions and a delightful man to deal with, but clearly not in charge of his department. The Brownites had used the loss of Labour seats in the election as a reason to launch a fresh internal assault on Blair's premiership. This had a paralysing effect on decision making because Brown regarded all spending departments, including Work and Pensions, as extensions of the Treasury and therefore himself. The Green Paper on disability reform, promised by Blair within weeks of the election, had still not appeared by the end of the year, the victim of endless turf wars in Whitehall.

Meanwhile, the summer was peppered with mini Conservative leadership bids as MPs looked in the mirror and wondered if they were not the one with the missing ingredient to beat New Labour. Most dropped out, and David Davis went into an early lead, but suffered the fate of many frontrunners as doubts set in and he made a poor speech at the October party conference. The party wanted a clean break with the past and the momentum switched to David Cameron, with Liam Fox in contention. I voted for Liam Fox, a tactical vote to try and ensure that the final runoff was between him and Cameron. Ken Clarke could count on the support of many of the old guard, but the new Conservative intake had shifted the party towards a position on Europe that more nearly reflected opinion in the country at large. Ken's support for the European Constitution, and his refusal to vote for a referendum on it, had been shown up by the French and Dutch referendum results as old fashioned and out of touch.

The second ballot eliminated Liam Fox, leaving David Cameron, who got 90 votes, and David Davis, with 57 votes, to go forward to a postal ballot of the whole Conservative membership. I voted for

David Cameron and urged my constituency membership to do the same. He was clearly a tactician, but on Europe he was unconditionally hostile to the idea of a European Constitution, agreed that the transfer of powers to the EU had gone too far, and seemed completely free of the Heathite baggage on Europe that had cramped the party for too long. He won the membership vote by two to one. The baton had passed to a decisively younger leadership, but Labour still had to be beaten and Britain's place in the world still had to be defined.

I joined the House of Commons Foreign Affairs Committee which was well staffed and carried out two or three substantial reports a year as well as keeping a continuous watch on the EU. I also became a member of the European Scrutiny Committee, which had the doleful task of sifting the vast quantity of draft EU regulations and directives that annually became law. Of course neither this committee, nor the House, could block such legislation or even amend it. The most we could do was get it debated and hope that someone listened, which was a sad state for a supposedly sovereign parliament. The European Scrutiny Committee sat in private, and even other MPs were barred from listening to its deliberations. I managed to force a vote on changing this, which we unexpectedly won, and for a few months the public had a right to see what was being done in their name by a parliament they had elected. The government then used their majority on the committee to overturn this experiment with democracy and the curtain was closed again.

The 'pause for reflection' called after the European Constitution debacle got longer and longer. Britain could have insisted that the constitution had failed and demanded a genuine effort at reform, but weakness and indecision prevailed and this allowed the centralizing dynamic of the EU to reassert itself. A 'group of wise men' was set up to find a way round the obstacle. This group was chaired by Giuliano Amato, one of Giscard's vice-chairmen, who naturally chose his old colleague, Jean-Luc Dehaene to sit on it as well. The group ended up with five ex-prime ministers and six members who had sat on the Convention, plus our own Chris Patten. They were the ultimate insiders. No dissident voices were included. No one was surprised when the group recommended that all the substance of the constitution had to be preserved, but repackaged. A few changes were proposed. The symbols of the EU, such as the flag and anthem and Europe Day, were dropped from the text. The foreign minister was retitled, 'The High Representative' but with identical powers. It was to be known as a Treaty not a Constitution. When he unveiled his plan at a press conference, Mr Amato put it candidly, 'We do not exclude that you reach the same final result.' The voters in the French and Dutch referendums must have wondered why they had bothered to vote at all.

Matters were not helped by the replacement of Jack Straw as Foreign Secretary by Margaret Beckett, in 2006. Straw was privately delighted by the defeat of the European Constitution as it saved the British government from a similar result. But he had annoyed the Americans by appearing to rule out air strikes against Iran in any circumstances, and Blair wanted a reshuffle. He also wanted to run foreign policy himself, as Gordon Brown colonized more and more domestic policy. It therefore suited Blair to have a weak Foreign Secretary like Mrs Beckett, whose foreign policy experience had been restricted to caravan holidays. She certainly made a poor impression on the foreign affairs committee when we first interviewed her, and under her the Foreign Office became increasingly sidelined, with all the important decisions being made in Downing Street.

Under the German presidency of the EU in the first half of 2007, the European Constitution rose from the dead. In March, the EU celebrated its 50th birthday and issued the Berlin Declaration, calling for more integration. It opened with the words, 'We the citizens of the European Union', but the document was only signed by the President of the European Parliament, the President of the Council, and the President of the Commission. The citizens were nowhere to be seen. I travelled to Berlin to speak at a rival event on the same day, organized by a German group called Mehr Demokratie, with speakers from ten EU countries. We issued an

'Alternative Berlin Declaration' demanding a genuine renewal process followed by referendums in all states. This event contrasted well with the Europe of Presidents meeting elsewhere in the city behind closed doors. I tried to get the BBC interested in covering our event, but true to form they stuck with Official Europe.

The German presidency, headed by Angela Merkel, adopted the Amato Group recommendations and moved rapidly to get general agreement. A leaked letter showed with startling clarity what was being planned. In it, member states were asked if they would agree to a new document so that, 'the Constitutional Treaty is preserved, with the necessary presentational changes'. It was proposed, 'to use different terminology without changing the legal substance'. Even Labour members were shocked by this attempt to dress up the constitution and disguise its intent. But Mrs Beckett went to ground and no minister would explain what was happening. Mike Gapes, the chairman of the Foreign Affairs Committee, wrote to her: 'The Committee regards the refusal of the FCO to provide a minister to give oral evidence during this crucial phase of discussions on the future of Europe as a failure of accountability to parliament.' The European Scrutiny Committee, also with a Labour chairman and Labour majority, complained that this secret drafting process cut out national parliaments and, 'could not have been better designed to marginalise their role'. All this from a government and a prime minister who had talked endlessly about the need for a new spirit of openness and engagement with Europe.

This particular piece of political manipulation was also Blair's last. He had become a liability to his party and his popularity had slipped badly in the polls. His refusal to call for a ceasefire when Israel had invaded Lebanon in 2006, aligning himself again with George Bush, had pushed Labour exasperation to breaking point. Under another complex deal with Gordon Brown, whereby the premiership was bartered between two men, Blair had agreed to go, and in June 2007 he went. Two days before he resigned he made a last statement to the House, explaining that although the substance and powers of the European Constitution were being resurrected, it was now to be called a Treaty and was therefore different, and no referendum would be held. It was a despicable exit.

Gordon Brown found himself on the right side of the door of No. 10 at last, and announced a blizzard of initiatives to try to relaunch the government. At the Foreign Office, Margaret Beckett was replaced by David Miliband, but EU policy remained the same. Portugal had now taken over the presidency from Germany and a few months later the Lisbon Treaty was agreed. In an act of symbolic grumpiness, Gordon Brown refused to attend the signing ceremony, and signed it later in a room by himself.

The Lisbon Treaty did not consolidate the existing European treaties into a single text under a single new body, as the draft Constitution had done. Instead, it amended the two main treaties – but the effect was the same. The government claimed that, because the word 'constitution' had been dropped, their promise to hold a referendum could be dropped as well, but in substance and effect, which is what mattered, the two documents were practically the same. This was proved by the European Scrutiny Committee which published a table comparing the two, clause by clause. The committee unanimously concluded that the European Constitution and the Lisbon Treaty were 'substantially equivalent'. The other select committee I sat on, the Foreign Affairs Committee, also looked at both documents: 'We conclude that there is no material difference between the provisions on foreign policy in the Constitutional Treaty which the Government made subject to approval in a referendum and those in the Lisbon Treaty on which a referendum is being denied'. The government's position had been exposed as a sham by the two committees of the House with expertise on the subject.

The government now had to get the Lisbon Treaty through Parliament, and in this they were greatly helped by the Liberal Democrats. During the Convention on the Future of Europe, Andrew Duff MEP, leader of the Liberal group and President of the European Federalists, had insistently argued for more EU powers and no national referendums. Some Liberal Democrat MPs were reported to be unhappy with this alliance with Labour, but Nick Clegg had just replaced Charles Kennedy as leader, and as an ex-MEP he was an uncritical supporter of the treaty.

The Lisbon Treaty was at root an old-fashioned document, making Europe more technocratic and centralized when the rest of the world was becoming more devolved, flexible and responsive. It did nothing to reform the notoriously inefficient EU budget, or cull the scores of hidden committees, or curb the impulse to regulate and control. It gave more powers to the very same EU institutions which had caused the problems in the first place. We critics were of course accused of being isolationists and hostile to European cooperation, but I saw the EU in a wider international context.

Britain has always had a dual character, the Continental and the Atlantic. General de Gaulle thought that our Atlantic tradition was dominant, making us unsuitable for membership of the Common Market. When vetoing our application to join in 1963, de Gaulle said, 'Britain is an insular, maritime country, whose nature, structure and economic position differ profoundly from those of the continentals.' Since then, membership of the EU took Britain politically towards Europe, while economically we were pulled in the opposite direction. It was claimed that 60 per cent of our trade was with the EU, but in fact over half of our foreign earnings came from outside Europe. And because we ran a large balance of payments deficit with the EU, we relied on the surplus we earned from the rest of the world, from investments, services and other earnings. The EU was becoming a low growth, high unemployment area with a falling birthrate, while the rest of the world was taking off.

At the same time, English had become the dominant language of business. The internet had opened up a vast new front in the global marketplace: its connections were Atlantic; its language was English. Distance had been conquered by electronic communications and mass travel. At the popular, cultural level, Britain was part of this global space, where the Anglosphere was more important than the European Union. Those worldwide connections of history and culture to which de Gaulle referred were therefore growing in importance and had not been replaced by a stronger European identity. This was not an argument for abandoning Europe, rejecting the single market or ignoring opportunities for European cooperation, but it did destroy the case for locking ourselves further into an exclusive European legal structure and exporting more powers to an unreformed EU. Because the EU was not just another international organization to which we belonged. Unlike the UN, NATO or the Commonwealth, it was primarily a law making body whose decrees were automatically superior to the laws of national parliaments. No other group of countries in the world had formed themselves into a similar legal structure, preferring instead to live, trade and co-operate on the basis of the free association of nation states. The Lisbon Treaty was a big step in the wrong direction; unwanted, unloved, against our interests, and mocking all the promises for a more democratic Europe in touch with the people.

The Treaty was 290 pages long, and 14 days were allocated for debates. William Hague led for us, ably supported by Mark Francois, the Shadow Europe Minister, who showed a similar grasp of the detail. The indefatigable Bill Cash, with his unrivalled knowledge of procedure, tabled dozens of amendments, and a small group of us attended and spoke in every debate. Large numbers of backbenchers, 84 in all, spoke in specific debates on the foreign policy parts, or justice or trade. To try to make the Treaty sound better, the government allocated one whole day to discuss climate change even though there were only six words on this subject in the whole document, and no new procedures to deal with it. On our side only Ken Clarke and John Gummer regularly attended to speak and vote against the Conservative line.

The government had relied heavily on the argument that the expansion of the EU to 27 members meant that the decision making had to be streamlined, with more majority voting and stronger central structures. In the event, enlargement went ahead under the old rules and no paralysis resulted, so that was another bogus scare. In fact the number of EU legal instruments examined by the European Scrutiny Committee was now running at over a thousand a year, making most MPs wish for a bit more paralysis. David Miliband's other ploy was to talk up the few concessions that the government had won, and imply that these alone justified the whole treaty. None of this could alter the granite fact that almost all of the proposals in the rejected European Constitution were to be enacted in this new treaty: the expansion of the EU into foreign and defence policy, the move into asylum and criminal justice, and with new powers over economic and employment policies. The EU would acquire a legal personality, able to sign international treaties like a state, and with an explicit primacy over the law of member states. The Charter of Fundamental Rights would become fully legally binding. Majority voting would apply in 38 new areas. The 97,000 pages of the accumulated laws and regulations of the EU, known as the *acquis communautaire* were untouched and were rolled forward into the new treaty. And to avoid the need for future treaty changes (with inconvenient demands for referendums), it was provided that parts of the treaty could in future be altered simply by agreement of the European Council. The treaty thus became self-amending. All this would cost money. Our net contributions, already over £4 billion a year, would increase to fund the new responsibilities, although the government refused to publish an estimate of the overall costs of EU membership, which were rising because of the escalating regulatory burden, the expanding EU budget, and the high cost of food because of the Common Agricultural Policy. There has never been an official cost/benefit analysis of our membership of the EU by any government, despite repeated requests.

As Labour members and their Liberal Democrat allies trooped through the division lobbies night after night in support of the Lisbon Treaty Bill, it was obvious that a referendum was the only hope, and we tabled an amendment that, if passed, would make ratification dependent on a yes vote in a referendum. The case was very strong. Parliament held its powers on trust from the people and was now proposing to transfer powers to an external jurisdiction. All the political parties had promised a referendum in their 2005 election manifestos. Labour would break that promise, but there were known to be a significant number of Labour backbenchers who would either abstain or vote for a referendum. The Northern Irish Unionists and the Scottish Nationalists supported us. It all depended on the Liberal Democrats, normally so keen on referendums. Apart from their manifesto promise, Nick Clegg had told the Lib Dem Party Conference, 'Any proposals which involve significant change in the relationship between the Union, the Member State and its citizens should be approved in Britain through a referendum.' Clegg had also called for, 'a new politics, of politicians who listen to people, not themselves'. After some days of speculation and rumination, the Liberal Democrats announced their decision: they would abstain. What they really wanted, so Clegg explained, was an in/out referendum on British membership of the EU, although this vote was denied by the Speaker as it was outside the scope of the bill. When the bill went to the House of Lords they were offered a vote on such an in/out referendum and the Lib Dem peers voted against, so they even lacked the courage of their lack of conviction. It is of course the birthright of every Liberal Democrat to be inconsistent and unreliable, but their abstention on the Commons vote on a referendum marked a new low. There were Labour rebels, and some Lib Dem rebels, but without the official support of Nick Clegg and the leadership, it had no hope and the vote was lost. David Cameron promised that a future Conservative government would hold the referendum.

The bill passed into law, and the UK ratified the Lisbon Treaty. But there was one more chapter in this shameful story. The Irish alone held a referendum on the Treaty, as was required by their constitution, and voted to reject it. As always happens, this was not accepted by the EU. The following year, 2009, Ireland was given some cosmetic assurances about the effect of the Treaty, a second referendum was held and the vote passed. By then, an economic crisis had hit Ireland which would expose deep flaws in another EU project, the euro.

Chapter 12

The Last Campaign

Gordon Brown's brief honeymoon with the British electorate ended when he planned and then cancelled a general election within four months of becoming Prime Minister. The author of a book entitled *Eight Portraits of Courage* was scared off by a successful Conservative Party Conference in October 2007. His attempts to distance himself from the Blair government never worked because he was largely in charge of domestic policy in those years, and his Treasury formula of tax and spend had so obviously weakened our ability to withstand the coming economic storm.

I took up some business interests, joining a health insurance company as a director and becoming chairman of London & Devonshire Trust, a property and housebuilding company. The outside interests of backbench MPs had become steadily more regulated and disapproved of, but they should have been encouraged. The rise of the full-time, professional politician had widened the gap between business and politics, while MPs were piling ever more taxes and regulations on businesses they had no experience of, and ministers were often amateurs at assessing commercial risk. For instance, Gordon Brown sold 400 tons of gold from the reserves at the bottom of the market, before the price went up fivefold, costing us over £15 billion. The period over which he sold the gold became known in the trade as Brown's Bottom. He was warned about this at the time, and when I later quizzed him about it in the House, he could only mumble that the sale had been agreed with banks around the world, as though that absolved him from taking proper advice or subjecting the plan to a thorough risk analysis, as any businessman would do.

Until one has been on the receiving end of stupid, job destroying regulations, it is all just a theory. When a planning officer delayed one of our industrial developments for six months because of some slow-worms discovered near the site, I wished he could have been on one of the visits I had just made to China, Japan and Korea with the Foreign Affairs Committee to see what we were up against. The real question was not whether one European country had different rules to another, but whether Europe as a whole was competitive in the wider world. We were paying a heavy price for the thousands of ministerial hours spent arguing over new regulations in Brussels. My favourite example at the time was the Physical Agents (Vibration) Directive, which was supposed to stop people sitting on farm tractors for too long. I gave it as an example at a conference in Copenhagen in 2002 when sharing a platform with Helle Thorning-Schmidt MEP, daughter-in-law of Neil Kinnock and later prime minister of Denmark. She attacked my claim and said the directive would not apply to agriculture, and, as rapporteur of the European Parliament committee which had drafted the legislation, she ought to know. In correspondence afterwards she admitted that agriculture was included. If people in charge of the EU committees forget what is in their directives it is not surprising that ordinary people feel alienated from the mysteries of how EU laws are made.

Meanwhile our global connections were being neglected. A British businessman in South Korea told us that when the president there was elected he got an immediate call from President Bush to congratulate him and remind him of the US commitment to South Korea, but only silence from the British government, and no ministerial visits. When we drove into North Korea we crossed the Imjin river, where the Gloucesters made their heroic stand against the Chinese forces in the Korean war, but these historic links, much valued by the countries concerned, have to be kept in repair by an active British foreign policy, not one that leaves it to the High Representative of the Union for Foreign Affairs.

The same visit was a chilling reminder that the fall of Communism was not total. North Korea, with its family dictatorship and nuclear weapons, was still technically at war with the South, and the border was heavily fortified on both sides. The North looked like a Spartan state – fully militarized with a million people under arms and the work being done by a helot class of workers. We visited a factory and saw some of them, sitting in unsmiling rows, filling plastic cosmetic bottles for export to the West, with their wages docked at source for 'living expenses'. North Koreans seeking refuge in China were regularly sent back to a dismal fate, but the Chinese government refused to live up to its obligations under the UN Convention on Refugees.

The Foreign Affairs Committee also visited Pakistan and Afghanistan in 2009 and reported pessimistically on the chances of military success. Britain had gone into Afghanistan to counter international terrorism and deny al-Qaeda a base, but this had gradually become a mission to build up the state, eliminate the drugs trade and establish human rights. However desirable these aims, they were not the reasons given for the original intervention, and the same was true of Iraq. Such wars are easy to start but without clear war aims they mutate into something different and are difficult to end. The Committee could find no clear set of principles governing these decisions, or any assessment of where the national interest lay. Our report was also critical of Pakistan, weak, badly governed and doing little to counter the radicalization of young British Muslims who travelled out there to attend the Islamic schools, or Madrassas, some of which urged holy war against the infidel.

The Committee visited America every year, usually New York and Washington where we were given good access to the UN, the State Department, Congress, the CIA and the large policy foundations. Washington was a marvellous city to visit: low rise, easy to get around, great buildings, and unusual in being the only American city primarily concerned with art and politics, not money. I always looked up Christopher Hitchens, who had made a life's journey from uncompromising Oxford Trotskyist to emphatic champion of US military intervention. Washington was an early dinner city, but Hitch kept British dining hours, so it was possible to attend an

143

official dinner with the rest of my committee and then go round to the Hitch flat for another one, where there was usually a combustible mixture of Neocons and unreformed lefties. Christopher regarded Islamic fundamentalism as a death cult, 'with us in its sights', which had to be halted by all available means. He was interested that the holy thorn, supposedly planted by Joseph of Arimathea in Glastonbury, in my constituency, had been cut down by Cromwell's troops in the English civil war to strike at the root of an opposing religion. He speculated that we should do the same to the Muslim Holy Places in Mecca. I don't know if he meant it; sometimes he just set out to shock. I agreed that we were challenged by a belief system which rejected the separation of religion and the state, but I doubted the effectiveness of military action against fundamentalism and preferred to strengthen the home base. Just as Soviet Communism was undermined by its own failings and contradictions, so these mediæval theocracies must in time give way to the internet age, the spread of knowledge and the human talent for self-expression and free inquiry. In Kabul, I visited a girls' school where 6,000 pupils were being educated in three shifts, and watched a science lesson in which a calf's heart was being dissected. These children were the hope for the future of Afghanistan – inquisitive, educated, and not inclined to accept the permanent second-class status allocated to them by the Taliban. Our report on Afghanistan recommended a programme of twinning between British and Afghan schools, which would be much more creative than the familiar and rather stale town twinning arrangements between British, French and German cities, which were subsidized by the EU.

Our reports on the Middle East underestimated the degree of instability in the region and its capacity to surprise. However we did comment on Syria's fake democracy, its malign interference in the internal affairs of Lebanon, and its craven support for Iran. President Assad's democratic credentials rested on his claimed 97 per cent vote in the recent presidential election, held every seven years. He was the only candidate. In Lebanon, we saw a sign of foreign interference from another quarter. In the south, hundreds of unexploded cluster bomblets from the 2006 Israeli invasion were lying in the fields, being defused by British experts, and the Israelis would not help by giving the numbers or likely locations of these fearsome munitions. I had seen the effect on civilians of anti-personnel mines in Cambodia: the amputated limbs, the eyeless children. Princess Diana was not a good royal consort, but she was right in her support for de-mining charities which make the ground safe again for civilians after the wars have faded from the news.

There were other visits – Turkey, Cyprus, Poland, Russia, Slovenia, the Czech Republic and the Balkans – and there were plenty of battles to be fought in the House of Commons as well. Labour's belief in big government was not matched by any idea about how to make it work. John Prescott, clearly with not enough to do as Deputy Prime Minister, had seized on the idea of directly elected regional assemblies, but his plan for one in the north east had been turned down in a local referendum by 78 per cent. Despite this, Somerset was forced into a meaningless South West Region, 200 miles long, and accompanied by a rudderless South West Regional Development Agency which spent money on some pet projects and a library of glossy brochures. Labour's next plan was to reorganize local government by creating large 'unitary councils'. This was enthusiastically backed by the Liberal Democrats but we stopped it by mobilizing opinion in favour of local democracy, winning a Somerset-wide poll on the subject, and bringing members of the Sealed Knot to London dressed as soldiers from Monmouth's Rebellion, to lobby the Department. The minister responsible wouldn't meet us, but a terrified civil servant agreed to accept the petition.

Immigration was a delicate subject, more often raised by constituents than by MPs in the House of Commons. On the Conservative side, we were not encouraged to give it prominence for fear of reinforcing our 'nasty party' image. In 2006, EU regulations were passed giving all EU citizens unrestricted and unconditional rights of residence in the UK, and access to education, housing and social security. This went much further than the general EU principle of 'freedom of movement'. The government objected to some of the new provisions, but was powerless to stop them as they were decided by majority voting. These new regulations were not debated in Parliament at all and this led to a revealing incident in the House. In the same month that these regulations came into effect, it was reported that over 1,000 foreign prisoners had been released without being considered for deportation. The row over this cost Charles Clarke, the Home Secretary, his job, and Tony Blair, in trying to recover the situation, stated in the House that in future, 'those who are convicted of a serious criminal offence are deported automatically'. But the EU immigration regulations that the government had just signed up to meant that no one could be deported to another EU country just because he was a criminal. So what the Prime Minister promised to do on immigration control was illegal under regulations his own government had just enacted. It was part of Blair's skill as a politician that he got away with this. The Conservative leadership was reluctant to exploit the matter because it conflicted with the party's rebranding exercise. We were told not to 'bang on' about Europe or immigration, and certainly not both at the same time.

The government had dramatically underestimated the influx of immigrants from the eight East European countries that joined the EU in 2004. The Home Office predicted a flow of between 5,000 and 13,000 annually; the actual figure turned out to be 427,000 in the first two years, 20 times higher. The European Scrutiny Committee did a study on this, and we travelled to Romania and Bulgaria to assess their fitness for membership in 2007. I wrote a pamphlet for Politeia, 'Who Controls Britain's Borders?', setting out the facts and putting the subject in an historical context.

The origin of the modern state could be traced to the 1648 Peace of Westphalia which ended the 30 Years' War, which was actually a series of incredibly violent religious wars in which civilian populations suffered worst of all. The Peace signalled the end of the Holy Roman Empire and created a system of sovereign, self-governing states which would decide their own religious affiliations. The Westphalian system has had many critics, particularly dictatorial empire builders. Hitler was a harsh critic, claiming it kept the German states weak and divided. The Soviet Union tore up the Westphalian system, and in recent times spokesmen for al-Qaeda have criticized it because it gets in the way of a universal Islamic Caliphate based on Sharia law.

Others claim that the nation has been made obsolete by globalization, with its distance-defying technologies, its international corporations and its huge monetary flows across borders. No state alone can control globalization, so the argument runs, therefore the system is dead and must give way to a supranational order. But the nation state was never all powerful. All of them engage with the outside world, by alliances and treaties, to advance shared interests and tackle problems. So the fact that a nation state cannot conquer global warming on its own, or defend itself without allies, is no argument for its abolition. What the nation state does do is ensure that international obligations, such as free trade or military alliances, are entered into on terms acceptable to its citizens, not imposed by external law makers. Nation states are necessary, indeed indispensible, for democracy. They give legitimacy to the making of laws. We agree to observe and obey the law because we control the way it is made. They are 'our laws', subject to scrutiny under a system of which we feel part, framed in a language we understand, and ultimately we can change or reject them. In other words, we belong to a unit, a community, which is appropriate for self-government.

So the sovereign state has proved remarkably resilient in every continent except Europe. It has repulsed the assaults of theorists and empire builders. It has not withered before the forces of globalization. Rather it responds to the human need for identity and belonging; for a sense of time and place; for democracy and legitimacy in government. It does this while allowing for the fullest possible international engagement and cooperation.

One essential attribute of this self-determining entity is that it decides who can settle permanently in it, and on what terms, and who qualifies for citizenship and in what numbers. In other words, it must control its own borders. My pamphlet showed that, for EU immigration, this was no longer true, and the transfer was designed to be irreversible: 500 million people from the European Economic Area had an unconditional right of entry, and this included an unknown number who entered other EU countries every year. In the last ten years, Spain had granted six amnesties to illegal immigrants from outside the EU. Italy had conducted five amnesties, France and Portugal held two, Belgium and Greece one each. All the beneficiaries would have an eventual unrestricted right to residence here.

Direct immigration to the UK from *outside* the EU, could still in theory be controlled but was heavily circumscribed by legal obligations under the European Convention on Human Rights, and all the case law that flowed from it. In addition, the Lisbon Treaty moved the EU more decisively into immigration policy. Britain and Ireland had a special arrangement and could opt into such measures on a case-by-case basis, and by 2007 had done so on 48 occasions. So our legal powers over immigration were either nonexistent or in steady decline.

It was not my purpose to judge the right level of immigration but to examine whether government promises about controlling immigration could be believed. Public concern about immigration was driven not just by numbers, but by a feeling that the system had broken down and no one was telling the truth. This could be countered by getting an administrative grip, but it also meant having the necessary legal powers. These were slipping away, and once powers are given away they are very difficult to retrieve. The situation was illustrated by a meeting I had with an MP from Bermuda. He told me that the island was having trouble with immigration from other Caribbean countries and had therefore imposed new restrictions. He asked if we could do the same and when I described our lack of powers he said what a paradox it was that Bermuda, the ex-colony and now an Overseas Territory, had more control over its citizenship than Britain, the mother country. He very politely suggested that perhaps Britain was now the colony.

With the Lisbon Treaty ratified, David Cameron dropped his pledge that the next Conservative government would hold a referendum on it, which caused a good deal of unhappiness in the party, and allegations of bad faith. But he did promise that the next Conservative government would work to repatriate EU powers over human rights, criminal justice, and social and employment legislation. This was a significant move as there was no provision in the EU treaty for any such transfer of powers back to a member state, so it was committing the party to a renegotiation of our relationship with the EU, with unpredictable results.

I was chairman of the European Research Group, taking over from Michael Spicer, whose steady good sense had been central to the eurosceptic cause. Members of ERG contributed financially so that we could employ a full-time researcher, which did something to counter the vast inequality of arms, whereby the European cause was promoted by government and EU money, leaving the euro-critical case to be researched by a handful of alternative agencies and think tanks. The ERG held regular breakfast meetings to keep in touch with these groups outside Parliament, including those in other EU countries where euroscepticism was in its infancy.

I was now regularly in the chamber of the House of Commons, but I noticed that the Speaker, Michael Martin, was not often calling me in debates or at question time. MPs tend to be paranoid about this, but Hansard entries confirmed an apparent bias. After an altercation in the House in which he seemed to lose his temper, I wrote and asked to see him. It was unknown for Speakers to refuse to see backbench MPs but he wrote back refusing a meeting. I remembered that when Matthew died I received many kind messages from Labour members, but not a word from Speaker Martin; yet when Gordon Brown's week-old baby died in the same year, the Speaker went to the funeral and made a statement of condolence. Speakers are supposed to cast aside party allegiance but Michael Martin was always intensely tribal. He eventually resigned over his mishandling of the expenses scandal.

An enjoyable side of the House of Commons is the range of all-party groups, on every subject from Accident Prevention to Zoos, and from Albania to Zimbabwe. I took on the chairmanship of two, the first being the British Museum Group set up to strengthen the parliamentary link with the British Museum, founded in 1753 by Act of Parliament, and today the finest such museum in the world. The second was the all-party Astronomy Group, established to promote space research and education. Cheap computer-aided amateur tele-scopes have made astronomy accessible to all, so anyone can see the moons of Jupiter, or the rings of Saturn, or can know that the light entering their eye started the journey from the Andromeda galaxy two and a half million years ago. I find that contemplation of the immensity of space, or the eons of time behind and in front of us, puts our fleeting existence and human quarrels into context and proportion. The main threat to amateur astronomy in England is light pollution which covers big cities in an orange glow and washes out all but the brightest stars and planets. Since the worst offender is the public sector, with its overlit buildings and often unnecessary road and street lights, I raised it repeatedly with environment ministers and even with the Prime Minister, but we continue to pollute the night sky, and waste energy at the same time. The environment is a fertile area for talk rather than action.

As the credit crunch of 2007 turned into the credit collapse of 2008, the national accounts disintegrated. This reordered all political priorities and moved economic management back to centre stage. It ended the Conservative flirtation with Labour economics which assumed that growth was permanent and that we had to match Labour's spending plans. The near collapse of the banking system gave Gordon Brown a fleeting boost but, as fear turned to anger, this was reversed and he became the target of innumerable plots from within his own party, all unsuccessful but all damaging.

In May 2009 a crisis of a different kind hit Parliament in the form of the expenses scandal. It had been known for some time that journalists were putting in Freedom of Information requests for details of MPs' claims for secretarial, travel and living expenses. I thought little about this as none of my claims had been queried by the Fees Office, and in total they were the lowest of the Somerset MPs. Before the matter of disclosure was decided in court, the *Daily Telegraph* bought a full copy of all expense claims from someone in the Fees Office and started to publish them, section by section.

The most lurid revelations concerned the 'Additional Cost Allowance' for the running costs and maintenance of a second home. This could either be in London or in the constituency. In my case, because I spent more time in London when Parliament was sitting, I designated my Pilton house as my second home and this had never changed. I did not charge mortgage interest on it, or anything from the so-called John Lewis list of household goods, but I did routinely charge for maintenance, both of the house and the garden. I also occasionally employed a man in the village who helped with the garden and sometimes brought in manure from his stable and spread it on the flower beds. Over the years this claim amounted to £388 and it was this that provided the irresistible headline, 'MP dumps manure on the taxpayer'. One journalist described it as the 'manure parliament'. It took its place alongside Peter Viggers' duck house and Douglas Hogg's supposed moat cleaning claim as exemplifying the whole flawed system.

Daily revelations about the claims of more and more MPs were extremely damaging to the reputation of Parliament. None of the expensive spin doctors and media advisors employed by the Conservative Party were made available to backbenchers. Four MPs and two peers were eventually convicted of fraudulent claims. The rest of us broke no rules, but the rules were lax and it was probably assumed by the Fees Office that the allowances were payable as part of the overall remuneration package of an MP. The obvious solution, to have fewer but better paid MPs and cut out the allowances, was never implemented. It was eventually decided by Sir Thomas Legg, who chaired an enquiry, to retrospectively disallow the bulk of MPs' cleaning and gardening claims for the past four years, and I paid these back without demur.

There was also an unwelcome late change to the Wells constituency boundary. An earlier big review of constituency boundaries had created new seats and abolished others, but Wells and its neighbour, Somerton and Frome, were left alone. The Boundary Commission then discovered that three local government wards straddled the constituency boundary. This caused no particular difficulty but the Boundary Commission decided to reopen the matter. Their revised plan took little account of local preferences and ties, but was adopted. Wells lost three rural villages that I had represented for 27 years and in return we got a village from Somerton and Frome whose political complexion was for me much worse. My agent, Mark Merchant, estimated that the changes would cost me 1,000 votes. Combined with the expenses scandal, this now put my majority at serious risk, but the Wells Conservative Association was working harder than ever and the executive committee wrote me a generous letter expressing total support.

There was another threat, which I thought I could remove. The UKIP candidate in Wells normally got about 1,600 votes, and most of these would otherwise have come to me. In a close election, this could cost me my seat. This nearly happened in 1997, and was certainly the reason we lost Somerton and Frome to the Lib Dems in that election. The leader of UKIP was Lord Pearson of Rannoch, who I had known for years and who knew exactly where I stood on the European question. He knew that I had resigned over the euro and that I was pressing hard for a Conservative promise to undo the Lisbon Treaty, with its unauthorized transfer of powers to the EU. When I saw David Cameron in his office I put it to him that our relationship with the EU was expensive, unproductive and corrosive of public trust, and that if he, David Cameron, was to be a great prime minister and not just a managerial one, he had to take this on and resolve it. His promise to repatriate powers over human rights, criminal justice, and social and employment legislation was an important step in the right direction. This would obviously require a Conservative government, and also MPs determined to make it happen. When I saw Malcolm Pearson at a party in January 2010 he seemed to understand that for UKIP to stand against such Conservative MPs in marginal seats was not a very good idea. At that time Wells did not have a UKIP candidate, so the leadership could have prevented it, as they had with other Conservative MPs in previous elections. But in the event Malcolm Pearson did nothing, and the local UKIP committee selected a candidate for Wells.

My Liberal Democrat opponent was Tessa Munt, who had stood against me in the previous election, lived in the constituency and was a full-time candidate. She had no special views beyond wanting every school to be a good one, every hospital to be a new one, spending to go up, taxes to come down, and of course no more tuition fees for university students. She also put out some vicious literature about my expenses claims, which was hypocritical as it later turned out that she was herself under investigation for wrongly claiming a single person discount on her council tax. People living on their own were entitled to 25 per cent off council tax, but the electoral register showed four men as well as Ms Munt living at the house she rented. This was spotted by Sedgemoor District Council and the truth slowly came out, although the Liberal Democrat commitment to openness and transparency was nowhere to be seen. The national press picked up the story later in the year, and the *Mail on Sunday* ran a full page on it, embellished with how one of the men lodging in the house was a Lib Dem councillor who, his wife claimed, was having an affair with Ms Munt. She eventually paid the sum back, but that was after the election. I broke none of the rules, but politics is all about timing and perception, and all this went against me.

Gordon Brown stretched out the Parliament as long as he could and the general election was finally called for 6 May 2010. Five weeks before polling day, I was packing up my office in the House of Commons prior to going to Wells the next day. The election was going to be called the next week but the whips had given us time off to start campaigning. At six o'clock in the evening I got a call from

Patrick McLaughlin, the Conservative Chief Whip, and went to see him in his office. He said that if I stepped down now as the candidate for Wells, I would go into the House of Lords.

It is not often that one gets an offer of appointment to another legislature, so I thought about it, spoke to Linda, and saw Patrick again later in the evening. They had clearly done some local polling and seen the damage that the expenses scandal was doing, and knew about the boundary change. Other more junior Conservative MPs had stood down and were known to have been offered peerages, but that was some months previously, when there was time for an orderly transition. In my case, we were just a few weeks away from the election. I had been adopted as the candidate for Wells, posters were printed and the canvassing was under way. If I now resigned, they would have to find a Conservative candidate within a few days and there had recently been a row in Norfolk where local Conservative members, the so-called Turnip Taliban, had objected to a candidate being imposed on them by Central Office. I felt that in all honour I could not accept the offer, and told Patrick that I had to refuse and would stand and fight; a mistake but one made from good motives.

The election was the most unpleasant of the seven that I had fought. In meetings at schools and colleges, Tessa Munt made great play of her pledge to abolish university tuition fees (a promise broken seven months later). I could only remind voters that, on the government's own figures, our national debt was rising to £1.4 trillion and it was irresponsible to add to it. Lord Pearson belatedly tried to get the UKIP candidate to stand down, but he was defiant and the publicity probably got him more votes.

For the Liberal Democrats, Nick Clegg and Vince Cable visited the constituency. There was also an extraordinary intervention by a group called 'Power 2010' which took out full-page advertisements to target six named MPs (three Conservatives, three Labour) who they alleged were, 'failing our democracy', and they included me. Power 2010 was funded by the Joseph Rowntree Reform Trust which had given £4.8 million to the Lib Dems and the director had just contributed a chapter to a book called, *Why Vote Liberal Democrat?* Their tests in deciding who had 'failed democracy' were about attitudes to Proportional Representation, reform of the House of Lords, opposition to ID cards, and whether there should be 'English votes for English laws'. Being a Lib Dem front, it excluded the question of a referendum on the Lisbon Treaty, which their MPs had promised and then reneged on. I had spent years trying to bring democracy to the EU, yet here was a group supporting the Liberal Democrats and accusing me of being anti-democratic. Groups of Power 2010 supporters visited Wells, dressed as cowboys and holding up 'Wanted' posters with my photograph on, all of which was reported in the local press. This campaigning was not covered by any expenditure cap, as the Joseph Rowntree trust claimed to be independent.

At national level, the Labour campaign was a slow motion car crash, which did not suit me personally as I needed the Labour vote in Wells to hold up. Nick Clegg had a surge in recognition after the first TV debate, in which he was bafflingly given equal air time, but this largely faded by the end. In Wells, I knew it was going to be very close and we kept up the campaigning to the very end. To those who expressed anger over parliamentary expenses I wrote a letter saying sorry for my part in it and pointing out that, of the 51 MPs in the South West, I had the second lowest expense claims overall, and the lowest in Somerset.

To UKIP supporters, I explained the obvious, that they would simply let in the Liberal Democrats, as had happened next door in Somerton and Frome in 1997. That would mean that a Conservative government was less likely, and I would not be there to ensure that election promises where kept.

As we drove to the count on the evening of 6 May, my agent Mark Merchant telephoned to say that a sample count of ballot papers as they were tipped out of the boxes was not encouraging. As the count got under way I could see that it was neck and neck or slightly worse. There were two recounts and then, at six o'clock in the morning, the result was announced. I had lost by 800 votes. The Labour vote had halved, UKIP got 1,711, and it was a Liberal Democrat win. After 27 years it was suddenly all over. Linda and I drove home in bright morning sunshine, and after two hours sleep I woke up, no longer the MP for Wells.

Chapter 13

What Next

As the whole of my middle years had been dominated by politics, it was not easy suddenly to return to civilian life, but I was lucky in having business posts that I could expand, and a family I could rely on. I told the Wells Conservative Association that I would not be seeking to recapture the seat. It was time to turn the page. For Linda, who was blameless in all this, it was especially hard to move house and start again, and I owed her everything.

Without an overall majority, David Cameron had to form a coalition with the Liberal Democrats. Old enmities were forgotten. David Laws, MP for Yeovil, who had attacked me for my expense claims, was found to have wrongly claimed a much larger sum for rent. David Cameron reluctantly accepted his resignation as Chief Secretary to the Treasury and said he hoped he would soon be back. The Standards and Privileges Committee found that Laws had broken six rules governing expenses and he was suspended from the House.

Coalitions work when they have a definite and urgent aim requiring a national effort, and this was provided by the economic crisis and the trillion pound national debt. But coalitions are not good instruments for governments in the longer term, since British political parties are themselves coalitions and government cannot for ever try to cover the whole waterfront. As it was, a number of election promises were junked, including the repatriation of powers from the EU, which was vetoed by the Liberal Democrats. This happened just as a central plank of the EU, the euro, gave way.

As noted, when an economic storm hits, what a country needs is flexibility and the capacity to respond. The countries of the eurozone were denied this. In joining the euro, they had thrown away the shock absorbers and given away their powers, and were now exposed to the consequences of their own folly. The pretended 'convergence' of the eurozone countries has been exposed as a myth, along with the 'no bail out' provision in the EU Treaty. The stronger and more competitive economies have had to bail out the uncompetitive ones, and as usual it is the ordinary wage earners who pay the price, not the politicians and eurocrats who got them into the mess. All this had been predicted; all had been ignored. At least I could take comfort from the fact that Britain was not part of this fiasco, and I had played a part in jerking the steering wheel to avoid it.

The task of building a better Europe requires those in charge unflinchingly to face up to past mistakes and abandon their automatic response to any crisis, which is to consolidate more power at the centre. The problem is exemplified by the euro project, which rested on two mistakes: one economic, one political.

Economically, the eurozone was never an 'Optimum Currency Area'. The differences between the participating national economies were too great, the mobility of labour between them too small, and the flexibility of wages and prices too low. In the absence of these, there was no transfer mechanism to redistribute money from the successful to the failing economies on anything like the scale required. This remained the case even after the 'no bail out' clause in the treaty was effectively abandoned in 2010. Nor were these obstacles temporary or transitional. The economies of Europe were not converging, and the gaps were getting wider. The northern economies continued to make productivity gains, but the unfortunately named PIIGS (Portugal, Ireland, Italy, Greece and Spain) lagged further behind, with poor performance, and wage increases which far outstripped productivity. Meanwhile, the European Central Bank encouraged the myth that the sovereign debt issued by the 17 eurozone member states was all the same, and equally risk free. This creaky structure was about to be hit by a hurricane.

The 2007/08 credit crunch exposed irresponsible borrowing and lending right across Europe and the USA. In the private sector, bankers had lent vast quantities of other people's money to other people they knew nothing about, collecting large bonuses while it lasted, and leaving the losses with the taxpayer when it failed. Governments behaved equally recklessly, with Gordon Brown repeating his mantra that he had 'ended boom and bust' even as the financial system imploded. Recovery from such a massive shock was always going to be painful, but, as Charles Darwin taught us, the organisms which survive are not necessarily the strongest but the most adaptable. The UK had its own currency, interest rates and monetary policy. Elsewhere in Europe, the straitjacket of the euro was a fatal handicap. Greece, the most exposed of the PIIGS, was insolvent and at the mercy of the markets once the flaws in the eurozone were exposed. Unable to regain its earning power by devaluation, it could only hope to restore its competitiveness by large cuts in wages and prices, which naturally ran into a storm of opposition at home. Big spending cuts, demanded by the EU authorities as a condition of support, further damaged growth prospects, making recovery even less likely. Imposing a savage deflation on countries unable to devalue does not solve an economic crisis or help repay debt.

Bail-outs were arranged and new central 'Stability Funds' were hastily put in place , but Germany and other creditor countries were understandably reluctant to take on an endless obligation to prop up the economies of southern Europe. As the tabloid *Bild* put it, why should German wage earners pay more tax so that Greek civil servants could go on retiring at 58? So a 'transfer union', whereby the weak economies would be permanently dependent on the generosity of the strong, was resisted. Instead, an EU 'fiscal union' was proposed, in which participating countries would give up their right to set their level of taxes and expenditure. The single European state would have arrived, though never requested or announced. This was the second mistake on which the euro rested: that the answer to every problem in Europe was to have more Europe. It was a familiar path. The collapse of the Exchange Rate Mechanism had led, not to an understanding of the limits to European integration, but to a still more ambitious project, the single European currency. When that got into trouble, the proposed solution was, again, more Europe and in March 2012 a majority of member states signed up to a new fiscal treaty to enforce budgetary controls from the centre.

Together with the provision of huge amounts of artificially cheap credit by the European Central Bank, this stabilized the situation, but did not address the underlying malaise. Centrally imposed rules on national budgets do not cure the problems of low growth and poor productivity. The structural weaknesses of the afflicted economies remain. Rescuing a country from a debt crisis does not transform work habits or the willingness of people to pay taxes, particularly when they know that the rich have got their money out already.

All this had been denied at the start. The 1990 European Commission publication, 'One Market, One Money', ruled out the need for centralized budgetary and tax controls. The campaigning organization, Britain in Europe, which was launched publicly in October 1999, with Tony Blair, Gordon Brown, Ken Clarke, Michael Heseltine and Charles Kennedy all sitting on the same platform, made the same point. They repeatedly denied that monetary union would lead to controls over tax and expenditure, and in the following year Britain in Europe published a pamphlet, 'The Case for the Euro', which mocked these concerns. The authors, Chris Hulne, Adair Turner, Will Hutton, Willem Buiter, and other savants, explained that each country would retain its own budget, which it would use to correct any disturbances and offset any shocks. 'That is, incidentally, the answer to one of the most widely held fallacies about the single currency: that it requires a large central budget in Brussels. It does not.' They were similarly dismissive of fears that the euro would require a fiscal union: 'Another argument employed against the single currency is that somehow it must lead inexorably to EU tax harmonisation. There is no logic in such claims.'

Were they all ignorant of the economics of currency unions? Or did they know the truth, but suppressed it? If the latter, it constitutes one of the great deceptions of the age. They certainly knew that there was widespread public opposition in Europe to the idea of giving up national currencies, seen as the indispensable repository of self-government and democratic choice. People therefore had to be taken there in stages, with the destination disguised and referendums avoided at all costs. This largely succeeded. In only two countries were the electors allowed a referendum on the single European currency: Demark and Sweden. In both these referendums the proposal to join the euro was decisively defeated. The Swedish result in 2003 was particularly striking as all the main political parties and business groups campaigned for a yes vote, but the entire country voted no except for one part of Stockholm.

This determination to build an ever more centralized union in defiance of public opinion is also shown by the way that the referendum results on successive EU treaty changes were circumvented. If a country voted yes to a new treaty, the result was unquestioned; if it voted no, it was taken as only a provisional expression of opinion and another referendum had to be held. Thus, the countries which voted no to the treaties of Maastricht (1992), Nice (2001), the European Constitution (2005), and Lisbon (2008), were ignored or told to try again. This contempt for public opinion comes at a price. It has created an EU which is all powerful in legal terms but politically stunted, lacking authority or respect. When the EU has to do something difficult or controversial, such as rescue its currency, it can call on no loyalty or allegiance. The workers demonstrating against wage cuts feel no obligation to save the euro, because it is not a project they ever approved or took ownership of. They could also see that the EU regarded the survival of the euro as more important than the survival of their jobs or their national economy. Equally, the German workers, whose wages were being taxed to provide the bail-out funds, feel no particular solidarity with Portugal or Greece, just because they are in the EU. It was different in 1990 when West Germany willingly transferred huge sums to the East to assist German reunification, based on popular understanding and participation.

CONFESSIONS OF A EUROSCEPTIC

The fundamental crisis in the EU is one of a lack of democracy. Successful political entities, such as nation states, are founded on a sustaining experience of some kind, such as a struggle for independence, a language, a religion, or a uniting cultural tradition. The EU has the claim that it arose out of a war-torn Europe and created peace. That overlooks the role of NATO in keeping the peace, but even if this is allowed, this rationale for the EU is losing its potency and is no longer adequate. Today's Europeans, growing up 60 years after the Second World War, are more global in their outlook and aspirations, while at the same time their instinctive loyalties are rooted in their own countries, and they want more choice and control over the institutions affecting their lives.

The Convention on the Future of Europe was instructed to tackle this but failed. The huge institutional bias towards more centralization was left untouched. The Laeken Declaration of 2001, which identified the democratic deficit, is still there, waiting for an answer. Yet, the eurozone crisis has taken the EU in completely the wrong direction. Instead of a simpler, more democratic Europe, 'closer to its citizens', it is proposed that the EU should centralize powers on an unprecedented scale through the creation of a 'fiscal union', with new powers to discipline countries and override national parliaments. The fiscal union would be a government which no national electorate could remove. So from one serious economic mistake, the euro, the EU is proposing to make a still more serious political mistake, the formation of a full political union with democracy further diluted. Greece, where democracy was first practiced, would be the first to suffer. A system which was supposed to bring Europe together, while avoiding German domination, has had the opposite effect of creating divisions and resentments, and deferring to German leadership.

At the European Summit in December 2011, David Cameron rightly vetoed the proposed treaty changes, on the grounds that they would be a threat to Britain's giant financial services sector and would infect the single market with regulations suitable only for the euro. The protection of British interests is indeed the first duty of any prime minister, but vetoes are not effective in isolation and have to be part of a plan. The outcome should be much more far reaching, giving momentum to a development which has been maturing for some time and which points to a different Europe, and a different relationship between Britain and the EU.

The guide to something different is contained in the unlikely phrase, 'variable geometry', by which the EU accommodates different groups of countries for different purposes. An alternative metaphor is, 'multi speed Europe', which in many respects already exists. For instance, the Schengen Agreement of 1985 abolished all border controls between EU countries, but excluded the UK, Ireland and Denmark. The defence provisions in the treaties make special allowance for traditionally neutral countries like Austria and Ireland. The Lisbon Treaty provided that some members could undertake 'permanent structured cooperation' for advanced defence. Then there is the Social Chapter, which was negotiated between most other countries, but originally excluded the UK. And the eurozone itself contains 17 out of 27 members of the EU. So a variable Europe already exists, with different states participating in different policy areas. This concept can be developed much further, to accommodate both the wishes of the eurozone countries to form a tighter inner core, and the desire of Britain to participate in the EU on different terms. The British veto was, at root, the rejection of an increasingly centralized EU, passing more laws in ever more policy areas, from which dissenting member states can only hope to obtain the occasional insecure 'opt-out'. The alternative is of a Europe of 'opt-ins', whereby countries, or groups, can come together for common purposes or to pursue common interests on a case-by-case basis. Such a change would never be accepted by most of the existing member states, but it is worth elaborating, as it could form the basis for Britain's relationship with the EU.

The only core functions of the EU would relate to trade, competition and the maintenance of the single market. Free trade agreements elsewhere in the world, such as NAFTA, show that this should primarily be about reducing barriers to trade, not passing endless harmonizing laws and regulations which cut growth and destroy jobs. The European Court of Justice would become a dispute resolution body, not a supreme court. The principle of free movement of workers within the EU would continue, but not as an unrestricted right to benefits and housing. The European Commission would lose its monopoly to initiate legislation and would become the secretariat to those national parliaments and governments wishing to launch cooperative endeavours or participate in joint programmes. Outside the core area of the single market, these opt-ins would be entirely voluntary, undertaken where member states wished to deal with cross-border problems or expand their influence by working jointly with other countries, on matters such as the environment. The EU budget would be cut to a fraction of its present size, funded by countries participating in each programme. For instance, if a country felt that its aid budget was better or more efficiently handled by the EU, it would pool it; if not, it would retain it. The same choice would exist for participation in the escalating number of EU quangos. Thus if a country wanted to participate in, say, the European Centre for the Development of Vocational Training, which is based at Thessalonika, it would join and pay an appropriate subscription. If participation in the European Asylum Support Office (in Malta) was deemed necessary, that could be joined too, but these agencies would cease to be a general charge on the EU budget.

Foreign policy would revert to being a matter between governments, which would allow a high level of discussion and coordination but without the expense of the unelected central institutions and the EU diplomatic service. The constraint on fashioning a single European foreign policy is in any case political not institutional. The search for an elusive 'European voice' on every aspect of world affairs is based on the belief, which is sometimes used to justify the entire EU project, that Europe must behave as a bloc, to stand up to America, China and the other great powers. Unfortunately, the pitiless struggle for influence in the world is increasingly dependent on economic success, and the EU's poor performance has undermined any dream of its becoming a world power. The sight of China being asked to bail out the euro should have punctured any illusion that the EU as an institution had found a way of meeting the challenge of the East. Foreign policy could happily be given back to member states and intergovernmental cooperation, without any loss to world peace and prosperity.

A Europe reformed along these lines would rest on the secure foundations of national parliamentary democracy, with powers conditionally given upwards for specific purposes, as happens under all other treaties. It would allow the inner core of eurozone states led by Germany and France to fix rules for themselves, which would not apply to non-euro states like Sweden and the Czech Republic. An immediate beneficiary would be Turkey, which has been negotiating to join the EU for over ten years but cannot fulfil the immensely complex entry requirements of the present EU, and is in any case likely to be vetoed by Austria and France. Turkey could far more easily join, and be accepted, into a more modest but enduring Europe of Democracies, based on the opt-in principle.

Without public referendums there is no chance of such a reformed EU being adopted, so the alternative is for Britain to apply these principles bilaterally, to obtain a relationship based on the ability to opt into measures on a case-by-case basis. These possibilities could include financial regulation, social and employment law, the environment, agricultural support, fisheries, research and development, aid expenditure and foreign policy. There is precedent for this. The UK already has such an opt-in arrangement in the field of criminal justice, whereby directives are proposed and discussed collectively and we then decide whether or not to participate. The only exception would be continuing full membership of the single market, or customs union, as it is desirable to preserve the free export of goods to the EU without the administrative complexity of 'rules of origin' tests. As most EU countries run substantial trade surpluses with the UK, it is unlikely that they would exclude us from the single market and thus see trade barriers erected against their exports.

These radical proposals would of course be attacked as an attempt to pick and choose, or dine 'à la carte'. But dining à la carte is what most people aim to do, and it is entirely legitimate for a country the size of Britain to design an 'opt-in' relationship with the EU which would respect the sovereignty of Parliament, and retain full trading rights. The background is one of continuing failure by the EU to tackle its democratic deficit or secure its economic future. Immense diplomatic effort has been expended in seeking solutions through the usual channels, to no avail. The Convention on the Future of Europe resulted in a European Constitution which was rejected, but enacted anyway. The EU is therefore not a successful, confident and democratic unit which can be scornful of change. Instead, it is an organization in crisis in which the public, if not the politicians, want reform. The euro crisis provides an additional opportunity because of the desire of the eurozone countries to form themselves into a fiscal union, while still using the institutions of the EU to enforce it. This gives Britain a potential veto, since the consent of all member states is required if, for instance, the European Court of Justice is to be given jurisdiction over a new eurozone treaty. Even if the countries concerned found a way round this by using existing treaty articles to set up new rules, the result is likely to be second best for them, and therefore gives Britain a great deal of leverage.

What is required is leadership and ambition. Europe will continue to torment British politics until a solution is found, and the circumstances are now favourable. The EU is not a force of nature but a man-made institution, and it is the job of politics to correct what is wrong and repeal what is objectionable. It is not healthy for the framework of British politics to be set by an institution which is so widely disliked and which has received no endorsement by the British people since the 1975 referendum, when it was called, on the ballot paper, the 'Common Market'. No one doubts the scale of the effort required, but it would be a liberating experience and its achievement would mark the start of a new era of cooperation and commitment.

The Conservative Party has already gone through the renegotiation barrier. Its 2010 election manifesto proposed to repatriate social and employment laws, and powers over criminal justice and human rights. As there is no provision in the EU treaties for repatriating powers in this way, it must necessarily involve an insistence; in other words a unilateral demand for treaty change. Rather than a piecemeal reform, this should be expanded into a comprehensive settlement to put Britain's relations with the EU on an entirely new and enduring basis.

The Liberal Democrats have vetoed the fulfilment of these Conservative manifesto promises, but they are on the wrong side of public opinion, and events. For instance, the coalition is agreed on the need for a 'growth strategy', realizing that the country cannot spend its way out of recession and instead must earn its way out by growth and production. This cannot be done without getting rid of expensive and job destroying business regulations. But most of these originate in the EU and have the status of treaty law which national parliaments cannot repeal. The coalition must choose between promoting Britain's economic interests, or clinging to an outmoded regulatory model imposed by the EU.

The arbiter must in any case be the British people. A draft treaty for change should be put to a national referendum, which would raise the matter above party allegiance or the short-term interests of the coalition. 'Staying in the EU for trade' would conform to what most people thought they were voting for in the 1975 referendum, while providing the fullest opportunity for wider cooperation and involvement.

Such a proposal would rally support from every point on the political spectrum. It is a mistake to regard criticism of the EU as being necessarily 'right wing'. The Labour Party was the only mainstream party to advocate complete withdrawal. New Labour and the Blairites did embrace the EU as a point of departure from Old Labour, and some on the left also saw it as a way of controlling market forces. But in this they were disappointed, as speculators made fortunes betting against politically determined currencies and exchange rates. Plenty of Labour MPs, and others on the left, retained their dislike of an organization which was contemptuous of democracy and put the survival of a monetary system above the welfare of working people.

Over the years I made common cause with people from all European countries and parties, in pursuit of a different, better Europe, truer to the ideals for which so many have struggled in the past. And when this great matter is put to the British people, as one day it will be, I have no doubt that the outcome will vindicate their efforts.

Political careers are largely unplanned, but if there was a thread which gave coherence to my time in the House of Commons it was a belief in parliamentary self-government and the need to defend it. Constitutional matters are important because they define how decisions are made and whom we obey. British history can be seen as a struggle to bring arbitrary power under popular control and it shocked me that Parliament was apparently willing to hand over powers that it held in trust, and to do this without losing a war. That it should do this to a demonstrably inefficient, wasteful and undemocratic body with a doomed currency, was something that had to be unswervingly resisted. I am content to have left that ripple on the pond.

Index